- that this
spires you.
Hannah Olivia
x

be healed be happy

A Journey to Inner Healing, Happiness, and Spiritual Wellness

Hannah Olivia

HEALING AND BEYOND PUBLISHING

Published by Healing and Beyond Publishing

Disclaimer

The information in this book should not be treated as a substitute for professional medical advice; always consult a qualified medical practitioner. Any use of the information is at the reader's discretion and risk. Neither the author nor the publisher can be held responsible for any loss, claim, or damage arising from use or misuse of the suggestions made, failure to seek medical advice, or reliance on third-party websites. The medical information included here is drawn from Hannah Olivia's individual consultation sessions, studies, and research. It is not intended to replace medical advice or treatment from your physician; therefore the author and the publisher accept no responsibility for any individual's interpretation or use of the information.

ISBN 978-1-9191985-0-7

First published in 2025 by Healing and Beyond Publishing

Contents

Good health and happiness comes from the peace
within your mind, body, emotions, and spirit.
It's important in life to understand that
we all have our own journey,
And whether that journey is good or
bad, totally depends on you.
You can choose to ride with the high exhilarating
waves or sink in the dark, deep, ocean.

Hannah Olivia

Dedication

To my parents, you've always been there for me, never judging my beliefs or the paths I've chosen to follow.

To my dear Dad, now in the spiritual realms of heaven. I know you've given me the energy, drive, and determination to follow my dreams and to write this book. You always believed in my ability to write, and from the very first day I decided to begin, I've felt your presence beside me, guiding me, and pushing me forward.

I've also felt my Nanny Glad and Omi stepping in energetically at different stages, contributing their writing skills and loving support from the other side. Thank you both dearly for being with me in this process.

To all of my spiritual teachers and mentors, both those I know personally and those I don't, your wisdom and teachings have truly inspired me.

To my divine healing team, my spiritual council members, ancestors, loved ones in spirit, the galactics, the angelic realms, and the elementals, you are the channels for the profound healing miracles I witness every day. Alongside the infinite power of God, it is your energy, guidance, wisdom, and healing that make these miracles possible. I tell my clients often: it isn't me they should thank. I'm simply the human channel for this extraordinary team.

To all of my clients who placed their trust in me and in the divine, thank you. Without the chance to walk with you through your challenges, I wouldn't have the knowledge or experience to write this book. Your faith in me from the very beginning has meant everything.

And finally, to my little family, you continually teach me more about myself, especially the parts of me that still need healing. Every day you help me grow into a better version of myself. I see so much of me reflected in you, and when I feel triggered, I recognise that you are my mirror, showing me what still needs love and healing within. The healing journey never ends; it simply transforms.

We need to learn to adapt to whatever the world throws at us.
Every experience is an opportunity to grow,
to accept, and, most of all, to love.
Love others, but more than anything, love ourselves fully.
We really can't truly love anyone or anything
fully until we hold love within us.
This is the key to inner peace, self-love, and acceptance.
The road to healing and happiness all starts with you.

Hannah Olivia

Chapter 1 – The Path to Healing

We have all gone through those tower moments at some point in our life. The moments when every direction that we look in appears to be crumbling in front of our very own eyes and we feel nothing but broken. All that we have learnt to be true and real, that we have nurtured and worked for, comes crashing down and our lives suddenly become painful and incredibly hard to cope with.

One minute we are sailing along the smooth current and the next, we are trying to dodge the tsunami and then we feel powerless. What these periods in our lives do is give us spiritual growth and take us on a journey of an awakening. They give us the chance to look deep within our soul and see what is out of alignment or not flowing in a positive direction, helping us to then travel on a better path in order to start anew. This enables us to grow foundations within us with a much firmer, greener, stronger and healthier root, allowing us to truly understand who we are and why we are here.

Giving us the opportunity to heal the parts of ourselves that have been buried away, forgotten, or neglected, and find the inner strength to flourish. What we once were, before our trauma turned our lives upside down, is no longer available to us. The old version of ourselves has no choice but to fall away. Even if this might feel uncomfortable and painful at first, it actually allows us the opportunity to test our endurance and gives us the room to heal and create something much more solid for the future. We become more resilient. We appreciate and grow into a much healthier version of ourselves because we begin to realise that at any moment in our present or future, we may well have to dodge another crumbling tower. These experiences prepare us. We start to appreciate the good times and live for everyday because we don't know what's around the corner. So rather than keep waiting for that special moment, we realise that in fact, the good days are happening right now. There is no waiting anymore. We learn to spend time healing the parts of us that were wounded or traumatised in order to live a more balanced and happy existence.

We are never fully healed, because healing isn't a linear process. New issues will continue to crop up as we go through new experiences in life. However, once we understand the healing process on our own individual journeys, this is when we can start to begin to accept and move through anything that is thrown our way. There's this ornate power within us that we never even knew existed but once we understand more about our energy we realise how powerful we truly are.

The more that we peel away at the layers of the orange peel, the more we remove all of the old energy attachments that we have been unnecessarily holding onto. These attachments from our past just make us miserable and physically restrict us from living a happy life. But once we remove all of those layers, it enables us to get to the juicy sweet ripe fruit. The happy content life that we have all dreamt of.

Sometimes we go through the most distressing experiences but I believe that every experience takes us onto a journey of enlightenment. Through the painful stinging nettles, we end up finding the healing dock leaves that take us into the exact direction and path that we always came on earth to fulfil.

A Little Bit of Background Information

In my early thirties, I was suffering from two chronic illnesses, tremendous hip and back issues and undergoing an emotional divorce. I found life overwhelmingly hard and debilitating. This period of my life made me go through immense questioning and soul searching. It transpired that I was born with hip dysplasia and hip impingement, that had not been picked up until much later in life. I had to undergo open hip surgery and went through a very long recovery process. But through this experience, my eyes really opened up to the different ways in which we can heal ourselves and find the true answers we seek to heal every layer of our emotional, spiritual, mental, and physical wellbeing.

When challenges are thrown our way, we have a totally different perspective on life. We can either choose to feel sorry for ourselves and wallow in our own self pity. Or we can embrace the challenges, learn from them, help ourselves, and in turn, help others with their own pain and suffering.

As soon as these struggles reared their ugly head, I started to acknowledge how my energy and these difficult experiences were making me feel and were affecting my quality of life and my physical, spiritual, emotional, and mental wellbeing. I wanted to find a way to move through these experiences and come out the other end even more powerful, resilient and strong.

The Importance of Understanding Our Energy

Rates of depression, anxiety, physical illness and even suicide are increasing to the point that we can no longer ignore the importance of our energy. Energy plays a vital role in our wellbeing. It influences the mind, body, spirit, and emotions, and when we truly understand it, so many of the issues we face could begin to heal.

Research released in 2024 by *Time to Talk Day* revealed that nearly two-thirds of people in the UK (64%) admitted to putting on a brave face rather than talking about their mental health.

Society often makes us feel as though we should just cope. Even when emotions feel overwhelming, many people stay silent because they fear that speaking up will make them look weak or powerless.

When we go to a doctor, we are often given a prescription, usually antidepressants. But medication can only mask symptoms; it rarely addresses the root cause. Most of our struggles are triggered by emotional imbalances within our energetic field, often connected to past or present experiences. These imbalances then manifest as mental, emotional, or physical issues. Depression doesn't just appear suddenly, like a visitor who comes and goes without reason. It builds gradually.

Negative thoughts carry frequencies, and over time, these frequencies manifest as low vibrational energies in the body. This creates a build-up of stagnant energy that weighs on our entire system long before we notice physical symptoms of depression. When the body can no longer handle this energetic pressure, depression begins to take root. If stagnant energy has nowhere to go, it transforms into illness, heaviness, and imbalance.

There are countless reasons why the mental, physical, or emotional body can fall out of balance. For example, a dysfunctional childhood may leave lingering trauma frequencies in your subconscious, continuing to affect you as an adult. A lack of self-love may stem from difficult relationships with parents, caregivers, or past experiences. These old wounds leave low vibrational imprints in your energy field, distorting how you see yourself and others. Until this energy is acknowledged and transformed, it can continue to create struggle. Healing requires shifting these frequencies from low vibrations into higher ones, so the energy can flow again.

Sometimes you may not even know why you feel off, or why you have persistent aches or pains. That's okay. What matters is the willingness to acknowledge that something within needs attention. Awareness is the first step toward positive change.

In my sessions, I often do spiritual healings for babies and children. Many parents contact me after exhausting all medical options, still unable to find the cause of their child's struggle. That's because issues can sometimes be traced back through the ancestral line, carried from parents, grandparents, and beyond. Children can even bring unresolved energy from the womb into this lifetime, which I will talk about in more detail in a later chapter.

Trauma, whether our own or inherited, can disrupt our energy field in ways we don't always see, but its impact is real.

Most people don't realise the enormous influence energy has on health, largely because we aren't taught about it in school or everyday life. Yet even our words and thoughts carry powerful frequencies. How we speak to ourselves and others shapes the reality we experience.

If we constantly affirm things like 'I'm poor,' 'I'm always sick,' or repeat stories about how hard life is, we reinforce those vibrations. Our energy lowers, and our environment begins to reflect it. But when we shift our words and thoughts toward love, gratitude and abundance, our vibration rises, and our reality changes.

For example, instead of saying:

'I'm unwell.'

you could say:

'I'm healing, my body is strong, and I'm becoming healthier every day.'

This simple shift aligns your energy with recovery and strength.

Think of yourself like a radio. When you tune into a station, you receive its frequency. Similarly, your thoughts tune into certain vibrations, and those vibrations shape your reality. Often without realising it, we create self-fulfilling prophecies. The more attention we give to a thought or belief, the more likely it is to manifest.

When we continually focus on negativity, the ego assumes this is our desire and reflects it back into our life. But we are far more powerful than we realise. We were born with free will, yet from childhood, society conditions us to hand over our power to schools, governments, and religions. It's no surprise that negative thinking feels natural, but with awareness, we can choose differently. You can shift your frequency in seconds by waking up to your power, trusting yourself, and remembering that the Universe always supports you.

If you keep saying 'I'm broke', then financial struggle will keep showing up. If you constantly complain about poor health, illness will remain in your field. Energy is always moving, either in a stagnant cycle or in a positive flow. Whatever we think and feel, we attract. This is why it's essential to focus on what we do want, not what we don't.

Once we raise our vibration, it's important to keep it steady by speaking positively, refocusing our attention, and choosing words that support healing and abundance. Otherwise, lower energies can creep back in and sabotage our progress.

One powerful practice is starting each day with positive affirmations. By affirming health, abundance, and joy, you reprogramme your subconscious and signal your energy field to align with those truths. Over time, this shifts old patterns into new experiences, keeping energy flowing in a healthy and supportive way.

The Energetic Impact of Our Interactions

We've all woken up feeling positive, only to find a few hours later, often after being at a crowded party, in a busy shopping centre or on public transport, that we're suddenly drained and out of balance. Often, we don't understand why. What has usually happened is that we've absorbed other people's stagnant thoughts and energies without realising it.

Everything is energy. This means that if the energy in our environment isn't vibrating at a high, positive frequency, we will inevitably feel it in our emotional, spiritual, mental, and physical selves. To stay peaceful and healthy, we must understand the movement and flow of our own vibration. When we do, we begin to restore our soul power, harmony, and vital energetic balance.

When we absorb the stress, frustration, or worries of others, or when we are in a room where people are arguing, criticising, or holding onto distorted behaviours, it wreaks havoc on our energetic system. It doesn't just affect us personally; it also impacts humanity as a whole. Every disagreement, even between just two people, ripples outward into the collective energy field.

If arguments carry anger, fear, or judgement, they attract and feed energies of conflict and separation. These energies then attract others, who carry similar frequencies across the globe. Someone already feeling stressed or wounded may suddenly feel heavier, more impatient, or quicker to lash out, without fully knowing why. This is why collective prayers and meditations are so powerful: they carry stabilising vibrations that can calm not just individuals, but even entire communities and cities.

So when you find yourself in conflict and you choose to shift it into peace, your decision is never just about you. That choice ripples out, calming your own energy and helping to stabilise the frequencies of thousands of others across the world.

Chapter 2 – What Is Healing?

How many times have you felt a symptom and immediately called the doctor or rushed to the nearest pharmacy, quicker than lightning, to buy a potion to fix it? We've all done it at some point, even if it was long before we began to understand more about our healing journey and the alternative ways to restore ourselves.

Many people in our modern world are not in tune with alternative healing modalities. Sadly, the systems we live in have shaped a society that often forgets our own natural ability to heal and the truth that the key to this power lies within us. It only needs to be unlocked.

There are countless powerful practices available to us, if we are willing to be open and acknowledge them. Yet, modern life has conditioned us to seek 'the fix' by visiting a doctor or getting a prescription.

From a young age we've been taught that this is simply 'how it's done,' and so it has become second nature. But true healing asks us to pause, to step back from this conditioned mindset, and to recognise the vast healing potential within ourselves. By tuning into our own bodies, we can discover profound wisdom about our health and emotional wellbeing. Alternative healing practices, many of which have been trusted for thousands of years, are here to guide us. We are far more powerful than we've been led to believe, if only we choose to honour the healing power that lives within us.

Shamanic practices are among the oldest spiritual traditions, carrying with them centuries of wisdom and alternative healing methods that remain valuable to us today. Through studying and learning from these ancient ways, I have gathered many tools that allow me to connect with the spirit world and support the healing of clients. Over time, I've developed a unique practice that respects and works with these ancient traditions, while shaping them into a modern approach to healing.

People often ask me, 'What exactly is spiritual healing and how does it work?' This is the perfect opportunity to explain more about energy and guide you into your first steps to understanding it.

At first glance, quantum physics and distant healing may seem like entirely different subjects, however they both explore invisible connections and unseen forces that shape our reality. In quantum physics, particles can be connected in such a way that even if they are separated by vast distances, they still affect one another instantly. This phenomenon, known as quantum entanglement, is like having two marbles that mirror each other's movements no matter how far apart they are.

Distant healing works on a similar principle. It is the belief that healing energy and intention can be directed from one person to another, even across hundreds of miles. Just as entangled particles remain linked, energy sent with purpose can reach and positively influence another person's body, mind, or spirit, even when they are not physically present. It's like sending a healing message through invisible channels that connect us all.

Although quantum physics doesn't directly work in the same way as distant healing, both share the understanding that everything in the universe is interconnected in ways that go beyond space, time, and our usual perception. Quantum physics explores this truth scientifically, while distant healing expresses it through spiritual practice, but both point to the same mystery of energy and connection.

I connect with my divine team from the higher star systems, such as the Pleiades, Orion, Lyra, and Arcturus. Each of these realms carries immense healing energy, and I often channel their wisdom through light language which is a beautiful multidimensional form of expression shared by the Galactic Councils. Light language flows through me in movement, sound, speaking, singing, and even dance, carrying vibrations that transcend the limits of ordinary words.

Alongside these connections, I also work with beings of the light, such as elemental spirits of earth, fire, air, and water; ancestors; beloved departed souls; spirit guides; and angelic presences. Together, they form a vast circle of support, offering guidance and healing energy.

Throughout my years of practice, I have woven these connections with energy work to create what I call spirit medicine. This includes universal prayer, visualisation, crystal healing, sound therapy, sacred symbols, healing codes, candles, number frequencies, colour vibrations, chants, and songs. In every healing session, I move energy within the mind, body, spirit, and emotions, and intuitively draw upon whichever tools or techniques I am guided to use in that moment.

When we think about the human body, most of us focus only on the physical aspects as we go about our daily lives. Yet as human beings, we also have a spiritual and energetic anatomy. This includes the aura, auric fields and bodies, chakras, meridians, heart and soul energies, as well as the energetic currents within the physical body. All of these are vital to our overall wellbeing.

With the support of higher divine forces, I facilitate the clearing and balancing of clients' auric field, physical energy, chakras, etheric energy templates, subconscious mind, energy cords, and any self-limiting beliefs that stem from past experiences. These imbalances can create disharmony within, which then affects how we feel and how we show up in the world.

Unresolved experiences can arise from many layers of our existence, whether from the present day, childhood, past lives, or even our ancestral lineages. These unresolved wounds often manifest as traumas or triggers that impact us physically, emotionally, and mentally. They can also interfere with our ability to create the life we desire, whether in love, abundance, success, or new opportunities, because they generate heavy, slow-moving energy that many describe as *blocks*.

I personally don't like to use the word *block*, as it carries a dense, low frequency and suggests something immovable, like a boulder in the way. In truth, energy is never fixed. It can always shift. With awareness, intention, and healing, you absolutely can move through and transform anything.

Self-limiting or self-sabotaging beliefs, along with destructive thought patterns, often need to be released before new opportunities can flow into our lives. When energy is stagnant, there is no space for fresh, uplifting energy or positive experiences to enter.

Some of this stagnation can even trace back to trauma from the womb or the birthing experience itself, which I've seen surface in many clients struggling with daily challenges or even issues around conception and infertility. At different points in life, all of us experience stress, anxiety, emotional turmoil, anger, resentment, negative thinking, and harsh self-judgment. We sometimes judge others too. Beyond this, we also absorb toxic energies from our environment, the food and drink we consume, the medications we take, and even the products we use. All of this builds up in our system and interferes with our essential magnetic energy levels, leaving us sluggish, imbalanced, and overwhelmed. When this happens, the nervous system becomes overly stressed, which in turn creates emotional, physical, and mental strain.

This is why it's so important to increase your magnetic energy daily in order to maintain wellness. Simply asking Spirit to raise your magnetic energy can create an immediate uplift. You may even notice yourself yawning or feeling a shift or shudder in your body as the energy moves through you, leaving you feeling lighter and more energised. At the end of this chapter, I'll share a simple activation you can use each day to strengthen your energy field.

When you really think about it, everything in the universe is interconnected through energy, and of course, this includes us. This is why energy healing can work across distances. It transmits in much the same way that a mobile phone transmits a signal to connect two people. Universal life force energy doesn't require physical proximity. My energy connects with a client simply through intention, by focusing on their name, visualising them, seeing their photograph, or even connecting with their face on a computer screen. Names themselves carry powerful frequencies, and our thoughts about another person create an energetic bridge.

Through this connection, I can tune into a client's energy frequency and vibration to facilitate distant healing. With the support of higher spiritual forces, prayer, and activation, energy flows through me and my hands. Using the many tools I've described, such as codes, symbols, sound, light language, and more, I help to adjust, clear, rebalance, repair, and transform non-beneficial energies into healthy, vibrant ones. In this way, clients can experience greater harmony, vitality, and emotional wellbeing, no matter where they are in the world.

Increasing Your Magnetic Energy Activation

Say this activation out loud with your hand placed on your heart:

Magnetic spirits increase my magnetic energy in my entire four-body system.
Keep increasing it in my mind, my body, my spirit, and my emotions.
Thank you God. It is done!

Now take a nice slow breath in and out, to shift any slow moving energy.

Notice how you feel afterwards. You may feel heat or cold sensations, a tingling sensation, or some kind of shift in energy as you say the activation.

We all connect with energy differently, but however you feel it, you will still have moved energy in a positive way.

If you didn't feel anything in this activation, do not worry. The energy would have still moved but you could also repeat the activation again if you feel that there might be some resistance not allowing the energy to fully move. If this is the case, then ask spirit out loud to release the fear spirit from your system. You can do this by saying the following:

Please release the fear spirit from my four-body system energy field and move it over to the light.

Then repeat the Magnetic Energy Activation again and notice if you feel a stronger shift.

Who Can Benefit from Healing?

I always raise an eyebrow when I meet someone who says they don't need healing. They look at me, baffled and confused, as if I've said something really insulting. If I'm honest, those are usually the people who need healing the most! In my opinion, every single one of us could benefit from healing in some way.

A lot of people practise emotional avoidance by walking around as though they have a positive mindset, when beneath the surface they are struggling. You could be the happiest person in the world but still suffer from health issues. You could be the most confident person in the world but still carry feelings of anger and resentment. Or you could be the most successful person in the world, yet still suffer terribly with anxiety and depression. How we portray ourselves externally is not always the same as what is happening internally.

From the outside looking in, you would never guess that some of my clients were struggling. Yet often the reason people don't thrive in life is rooted in feelings of unworthiness. Feelings that are linked to traumas or triggers from both the past and the present. By healing and clearing these issues within the subconscious mind and energetic field, those heavy patterns begin to shift, allowing for a more fulfilling, balanced, and healthier future.

I have worked with many highly successful clients, yet even they had areas of life in need of healing. This is because healing is never linear. It is a lifelong journey that unfolds in waves, sometimes gentle, sometimes powerful, and always ongoing.

We all face testing times, but not all traumas originate in this lifetime. I talk about past lives in more detail later on, but just to touch on it briefly. Whether or not you personally believe in past lives, there is much research, as well as evidence from my own work, that shows unresolved wounds can be carried from one life to the next. These issues may also come through our families, passed down the ancestral line, embedding themselves in our energetic field. If they remain unaddressed, they continue to fester, resurfacing again and again until they are healed.

Years ago, before I understood my own intuitive power to access different timelines, I experienced past-life regression sessions. They revealed striking connections between challenges in my present life and experiences from other lifetimes, as well as patterns running through my family lineage. Through mediumship training, I also came to understand that many of us choose specific experiences before we are born, sometimes even painful ones, in order to grow, evolve, and transcend.

This can feel like a hard truth to accept, especially if you've endured deep trauma. But sometimes, what we face in this lifetime is connected to something we once caused in another. We may choose to return and experience life on 'the other side of the coin', not as punishment, but as a path towards understanding, empathy, and ultimately, evolution. Life gives us free will, and we can choose to stay trapped in suffering, or we can choose to rise above it and allow those experiences to transform us.

When we avoid our pain, leaving issues to fester, they only grow stronger. Imagine going on holiday and forgetting about a half-eaten loaf of bread in the bread bin. At first, a few patches of mould appear, but if left unchecked, the mould eventually consumes the entire loaf until it disintegrates. The same is true for unhealed energy within us. If we don't address emotional wounds, they spread quietly through our mind, body, spirit, and emotions, eating away at our vitality until we feel fragmented and depleted.

Every unresolved trauma eventually creates triggers, which lead to distress, unhappiness, and health challenges. Our emotions must find a way out. If we ignore them, the body will eventually speak for us, sometimes gently, sometimes loudly, until we can no longer overlook what needs to be healed.

What Can We Heal?

Here are just a few of the issues clients have come to me with, so that they can heal and move energy within their system.

I have even eradicated chemicals, metals such as lead, mercury, arsenic, aluminium, ammonia, chloride, fluoride, and cadmium, as well as other toxins and radiation from the body, whether from vaccines, medication, food, drink, or the environment, which have caused disturbing and unwanted effects on the body. My spiritual team has also assisted me in creating spiritual intravenous drips to provide vitamins, minerals, and other beneficial treatments to my clients' bodies.

Ailments That Have Been Improved or Cured Through Spiritual Healing

- Eating issues
- Weight issues
- Money issues
- Mental health issues - anxiety, depression, bipolar etc
- ADHD issues
- Autism issues
- Panic attacks
- Behavioural issues
- Physical issues and pain
- Fertility
- Viruses alongside other illnesses
- Colic and reflux
- Insomnia and sleep disturbances
- Allergies
- Addictions
- Compulsive disorders
- Self harming
- Relationship issues including family discord

- Financial issues
- Career issues
- Self confidence, belief and self esteem issues
- Sadness and depression
- Anger and frustration
- Impatience
- Skin issues
- Fear
- Physical pain
- Tumours
- Ingrown hairs
- Cysts

The Power of Healing and Its Impact on the Mind

I am a true believer that the first step in any healing journey is acknowledging that we all need healing, whether emotionally, mentally, or physically. This recognition is often the catalyst for transformation. On a subconscious level, without even realising it, we begin to feel lighter and happier because we have set ourselves free. Simply taking that initial step forward can shift a person's mindset remarkably quickly.

The importance of a positive mindset, belief, and appreciation cannot be overstated. These frequencies are incredibly powerful. They can move mountains in our reality. The effectiveness of prayer, combined with the universal energy, is phenomenal in its ability to heal and transform on every level: quantum, spiritual, and shamanic. Yet so many people remain unaware of these modalities or their profound benefits. If they were to explore them, they would discover a natural and deeply transformative way to heal many areas of their lives.

We are all interconnected. Every living being on this Earth shares an energetic bond. Yet many humans feel separated from this truth, and it is not entirely their fault. Society, education, and cultural conditioning have taught us that humans, animals, and all living things are separate. Our connection to the spirit world, higher dimensions, and even concepts like reincarnation is rarely acknowledged in schools or religious teachings. Spirituality is often dismissed or even labelled dangerous, leaving many of us disconnected from our own inner power.

The matrix and hierarchical systems benefit from keeping this knowledge hidden. They see awakened, empowered individuals as a threat. But once I realised that all power resides within me, and that external validation was unnecessary, my life changed profoundly. Everything became easier. I believe the world would be vastly different if children were taught from a young age about energy, spiritual connection, and the power within themselves. Instead, we are taught to conform, judge, and separate; to believe that some things are right, others wrong, and that deviation from the system is corruption.

Fear, separation, lack of faith, and the belief in human hierarchy dominate much of society. But in truth, we are all equal, powerful, and loving beings. When we heal ourselves, it has a ripple effect. Our energy impacts those around us and the world at large. Healing is never just personal; it contributes to collective healing, including the energy of Mother Earth. Love is the highest force in existence. Even when I have never met a client, even if they live thousands of miles away, the energetic love transmitted through my thoughts, words, visualisation, and intention can create profound miracles.

I am guided by my intuition, my divine healing team, and my spiritual council to address the root cause of each issue. Every day, I witness miraculous healing in my clients, and much of this power comes from belief, trusting in the process, and the alignment of mind, body, spirit and emotions. When we choose to heal ourselves consciously, we are not only transforming our own lives but contributing to the healing of the world.

Chapter 3 – Religion, Spirituality, and the Matrix of Control

When you take the matrix's programming out of the equation, what comes to mind when you think of religion and spirituality? Do you see them as the same, or completely different?

I've spoken to people who fear that exploring spirituality will interfere with their religious beliefs, so they shy away from healing or learning about energetic practices. Some even feel that engaging in spiritual practices would betray God or their place of worship. This couldn't be further from the truth. As I mentioned in the last chapter, these fears were instilled by a system designed to suppress human power, teaching society that unless authority figures like priests or preachers guide us, we will be punished by God.

Systems like this are dangerous because they prevent us from trusting our intuition and divine guidance, which is far more natural and aligned with the soul. Instead, we conform to prescribed beliefs, often without question. Throughout history, those, particularly women, who sought personal power by using spiritual healing abilities were often persecuted and labelled as witches. Many were even killed for their gifts. Even today, the negative portrayal of witches in stories and media reinforces this fear, teaching us that mystical power is dangerous or wrong.

Those in power, intentionally created systems of doubt to stop us from realising our full human potential and discovering alternative ways to heal. Modern society continues to discourage the exploration of natural healing methods because it threatens industries like pharmaceuticals, which profit from keeping us dependent on medication.

The truth is, every single one of us has the power to create magic and transform our lives. Many of us have forgotten this power, or push it away out of fear of judgment or misunderstanding. A fear often rooted in experiences from past lifetimes (I explore past lives further in chapter 5). False belief systems, passed down through generations, have limited our understanding of ourselves.

Religion, in essence, is an institutionalised system of beliefs and practices, centered on worship and obedience to a higher authority. Spirituality, on the other hand, is personal, flexible, and empowering. It has no hierarchy, no punishment, and no rigid rules. In spirituality, you understand that God, or the universal life force, is within all of us. Nothing that happens in your life is a punishment from God; rather, it is a reflection of the energetic reality we create with our thoughts, words, and actions.

Spirituality connects us to something greater than ourselves. It helps us find purpose, navigate life's challenges, and embrace authenticity, love, and acceptance. It encourages us to learn and grow without judgment, knowing that divine energy is ever present and supportive.

Despite so much conflict over religion in the world, most people share a common desire: to connect with a higher force, aspire to kindness, and live as the best version of themselves. Division, hate, and war often stem from those in power, who benefit from keeping humans separate and fearful. In my view, this is one reason why religions have been structured the way they are.

Spirituality is broad, personal, and can mean different things to different people. Some people choose to practice both religion and spirituality, finding that they can coexist harmoniously. Spirituality, however, does not impose guilt, hierarchy, or punishment. There is no hell. When we transition from this earthly life, we return to the spirit world to review our experiences and lessons. Where we go in the spirit realms depends on how we lived, the lessons we embraced, and the growth we achieved. We continue to evolve, learning from mistakes, and return to the earthly plane if we choose, for another soul experience.

Many studies and books explore these ideas. Michael Newton, Ph.D., has conducted extensive case studies in his own books on the different spiritual realms, providing evidence of the soul's eternal journey. From my own research and experience, I have found that every challenge, every connection, and every interaction we experience is part of our ongoing learning, even beyond this physical life. Our body is merely a biological *spacesuit*, while the soul continues to grow, evolve, and expand infinitely.

If you want to look into this in more detail, the spiritual teacher and author Dolores Cannon has written extensively about these truths through her channeled messages and findings. Her work offers a deeper understanding of the soul's journey, reincarnation, and the higher dimensions.

In many religious practices, the concepts of heaven and hell are central, with the belief that once we die, we do not return. But from my studies, experiences, and countless past-life regression sessions, I have come to a very different understanding. I believe that our soul is eternal, and if it chooses, it can return to experience another lifetime again and again. Each incarnation is an opportunity to learn, grow, evolve, and transcend.

Books such as *Life Before Life* and *Return to Life* by Dr. Jim B. Tucker further support these ideas. I have seen too many glimpses of my own past lives to believe otherwise. I also believe there are different levels within the spirit world, and where we find ourselves after death depends not on punishment from God, but on the choices and energies we projected during our lifetime. The only true hell is the one we create within our minds.

I didn't grow up in a spiritually minded family. I was raised Christian. I still hold respect for Christianity and many other religions, not for their hierarchy or rigid rules, but for their foundations in love, faith, and resilience. When I think of Jesus, I see a healer who embodied compassion, selflessness, and forgiveness. He gave his time and energy freely, without judgment, and lived fully by his truth. Whether religious or not, we cannot deny the profound impact of his example to the world.

I make no judgment on what others choose to believe. What saddens me is not faith itself, but the systems that manipulate it. Humanity was given free will, but far too often we forget this and allow others to dictate our thoughts, beliefs, and choices. These limitations then get passed down to the next generation, and so the cycle continues.

In my healing practices, I often work with God, the angelic realms, and sometimes with Jesus, Mother Mary, and Mary Magdalene. Their energy is powerful, compassionate, and filled with love. Yet I do not align with all religious rules, because many of them do not resonate with my spiritual understanding. I have always kept an open mind and an open heart. I believe in God, I know Jesus is real, and I experience the angels daily. Like many spiritual people, I connect to these higher beings not through hierarchy or ritual, but through love, intention, and devotion.

I have been blessed with angelic encounters at key moments in my life, once while travelling to work on a train, and another time in my bedroom after losing a baby. I know I was meant to see them at those exact times, as preparation for the work I would one day do.

I hold deep respect for the values of Hinduism, Sikhism, Buddhism, and many other faiths. Many of these traditions emphasise forgiveness, compassion, and unconditional love. They teach that the soul is eternal, an understanding that resonates strongly with spirituality. While religions differ on whether the soul reincarnates, spirituality embraces the truth that our soul continues beyond this physical form. Each time we return, we wear a new *biological suit*, but the soul itself never changes. It is eternal, evolving through each experience.

This is why I see spirituality as an integration of the positive values across religions, without the judgment, fear, or control of hierarchical systems. Spirituality reminds us that God does not punish us, because we are part of God. We do not need to beg for forgiveness, for divine love is unconditional and ever present. The world was never created to divide us into categories of belief, it was created for love, acceptance, and unity.

Sadly, many people feel trapped by the expectations of their religion, families, or communities. I have experienced sessions with clients who live in fear of expressing their true selves, their sexuality, their beliefs, or their passions, because of how others might judge them. This suppression often leads to emotional, mental, and even physical health issues. When we are authentic, we feel free, but when we deny our truth, we live in constant disconnection.

For me, spirituality is about wholeness. It is the recognition that we are more than our bodies. We are eternal beings capable of joy, peace, healing, and love. It is about breaking outdated ancestral patterns and teaching the next generation new ways of living with openness, compassion, and authenticity.

We all arrive on Earth at different stages of our soul's evolution, but no one is more special than another. We simply forget who we are and what we've learned across lifetimes. A spiritual path helps us remember, bringing healing, empowerment, and a deeper understanding of our purpose.

Of course, our journey is not without challenges. We live in a world of polarity, light and dark, joy and pain. The key is not to fear or suppress the darkness, but to acknowledge it, learn from it, and transcend it. When we do, the results are profound.

We must also remember that not everyone who claims to be spiritual, loving, or enlightened is genuine. Just as in religion, there are those who misuse their power or act from ego rather than love. This is why discernment is essential. By listening to our intuition and feeling into the energy behind people's words and actions, we can recognise authenticity and choose wisely who we allow to guide or influence us.

The Power of Prayer Activation

I understand that some readers might not be religious or feel comfortable with prayer, and I've always respected everyone's views and their right to believe whatever resonates with them. Even if you don't resonate with the idea of God, I believe you will still feel that there is some kind of higher force or greater existence beyond our little planet. With this understanding, you'll begin to realise just how powerful energy is, and how potent prayer and activation can be.

After all, prayer is likely as old as humanity itself. People of every race, culture, and gender pray around the world in countless forms and traditions. When we examine prayer more deeply, we see that it is both a science and an art to experience. It is powerful, but you must understand how to pray. I know this from experience: I used to pray in ways that were completely ineffective and often wondered why I wasn't seeing results.

Effective prayer does not necessarily require belief in a specific deity or religion. Yet many people go to religious settings, praying and begging for forgiveness, only to feel frustrated when their prayers seem unanswered. This is because the principles of prayer and pre-activation are often misunderstood. When certain aspects of prayer are done incorrectly, they can lose much of their power.

Prayer is central to religious practices worldwide, but it is also an important part of my daily spiritual healing work. In my experience, it is one of the most powerful tools available. I have had sessions with clients who would never have considered incorporating prayer into their lives, but after spending time together, they saw how transformative it could be. When a prayer is delivered with clarity, intention, is specific, and holds full belief, trust, and feeling in every word, it becomes incredibly effective.

During my healing sessions, I connect both with the client's energy and my own through prayer activations. I call upon specific angels, ancestors, spirits, and higher forces to intervene and assist with healing, but never override a client's free will. When prayer is approached correctly, it is a sacred co-creation with the universe, and creates powerful results.

Key Tips to Successful Prayer Activations

- **Stay present and believe**. Trust that what you are asking Spirit for has already manifested into your reality.
- **Pray from the heart**, really feeling the frequency of your words with the requested prayer.
- **Be clear in your intent and vision.**
- **Choose your words carefully**. Every word carries a frequency, so it's crucial to be mindful of your selection.
- **Have faith**. Don't allow doubt or lack to creep in. Often, lower vibrations like doubt, negativity, distrust,

and scarcity are created by matrix programming. Be aware of where your thoughts are going.

- **Do not beg**. Begging sends frequencies of lack, distrust, and desperation. For example:

God please don't punish me!

This portrays God as angry and separate from us. Yet God, or a higher force, is within us all and is never angry. We only feel separation through our own emotions.

- **Never wish harm on others**. Wishing harm divides humanity into good and bad and blocks oneness. For example:

God, please punish this person for what they have done to me.

Remember: **cause and effect**. If you wish harm, it will return to you tenfold.

- **Avoid negative or frustrated prayers. For example:**

Help me. Life is such a struggle and I'm sick. Why aren't you listening?

This energy brings despair, anger, and lack of trust, weakening the power of your prayer.

- **Show appreciation and gratitude**. Saying 'thank you' aligns your energy with positive frequencies and allows more good to flow into your life.
- **Pray with 'You are.'**

Soul, you are healthy! Thank you God.

This speaks directly to your soul, which is more powerful than Saying *I*. You are affirming health and belief in a positive outcome. Speaking to *you* addresses the child within, who listens and receives without filters.

- **Use repetition, rhythm, and mantras**. Repeating specific words builds energy and momentum. Mantras amplify the frequency of your prayer.
- **Surrender the outcome**. Avoid attaching to results or projecting lack or doubt. Say things like:

It is done! Or I say yes to this!

Yes dissolves resistance and is the language of the universe. Affirming it shows you are ready to receive, then let go and trust.

- **Take action when necessary**. Prayer is powerful, but you may also need to meet Spirit halfway. For example, if you are sick:
- Improve your diet.
- Avoid foods with chemicals or toxins.
- Stay positive instead of wallowing in self-pity.
- Ask yourself if you truly want to live.

Similarly, for career goals:

- Update your résumé or curriculum vitae.
- Take courses to align your skills with your goals.
- **Trust divine timing**. The universe will align prayers for your highest good. Some prayers, which I call *spiritual activations*, shift energy instantly, and results can appear within seconds.

Prayer Activation Exercises

Below are some examples of prayers and spiritual activations that you can explore to support yourself. As you become more comfortable playing with these activations, you can create your own that resonate with your unique needs.

Take a moment to look at the key tips above to guide you in creating powerful and successful prayer activations. If you are not religious or feel uneasy using the word *God*, feel free to replace it with terms such as *Thank you, Universe or Thank you, higher dimensions/realms,* or any expression that truly feels right for you.

When using the following activations, you can speak them aloud or silently in your mind. You might like to place your hand over your heart, or somewhere else on your body that feels natural, to help you connect with the energy. Allow yourself to feel the words as they flow, and let the experience be gentle, personal, and uplifting.

Prayer 1 Activation – Clearing Energy

I ask the seven archangels of God's divine light to clear all non-beneficial energies from my mind, body, spirit, soul, aura, and etheric energy template that no longer serves me or causes imbalance.
I am cleared.
Thank you, God.
Amen.
It is done!

Tip: Place your hands over your heart and take three deep, slow breaths before saying the prayer. Visualise a white or golden light sweeping through your body, mind, and aura, clearing anything that doesn't serve you.

Prayer 2 Activation – Healing for the World

Spirits of light, love, peace, and harmony, please bless the Earth with infinite loving frequencies. Send the highest form of light to any dark areas in disharmony, and fill them with peace, love, hope, and healing. Thank you, God. Amen. It is done!

Tip: Picture the Earth glowing with radiant light. Imagine the light touching every person, animal, and place in need. Feel your intention expanding outward with love and compassion.

Prayer 3 Activation – Home Healing

Please bless my home with divine light. Invite spirits of love, light, and balance to move any stagnating energies or lower vibrations. Ignite light energies in every room, creating harmony and peace. I am at peace in my home, and it is filled with love. Thank you, God. Amen. It is done!

Tip: Walk through each room slowly, either physically or in your mind, imagining a warm, glowing light filling the space. You can place your hands on a wall or surface and visualise the light spreading from your touch.

Prayer 4 Activation – Clearing Radiation and Toxins/ chemicals from the Body

I ask infinite love to clear all non-beneficial chemicals, metals, toxins, and radiation from my body, including lead, mercury, arsenic, aluminium, ammonia, chloride, fluoride, and cadmium. I am clear, and my energy field and body are pure. Every cell within me is at peace. My nervous system is calm and clear. Thank you, God. It is done!

Tip: Sit or lie comfortably and place your hands over the areas you want to clear, or simply on your heart. Breathe slowly, imagining the toxins being lifted and replaced with pure, healing light. Feel your cells relaxing and glowing with energy.

Create Your Own Prayer Activations

Take a moment to tune into your heart and intuition. Write your own prayers in the space below or in your personal notebook. Feel free to use your own words, your own intentions, and your own visualisations. Notice the energy shift as you create prayers that are uniquely yours.

1. ____

____

____

____

____

____

____

2. ____

____

____

____

____

____

____

____

3. ____

____

____

____

____

____

____

____

4. ____

____

____

____

____

____

____

How to Create Affirmations in a More Powerful Way

Affirmations have become a very popular trend in society and in new age spiritual practices. Many people find that saying affirmations feels like a more comfortable way of connecting with a higher source without the need for prayer. I personally feel, however, that most of us haven't been taught how to truly connect on a deeper level with the energy of the words we use in affirmations.

In much of the new age spiritual community, affirmations are taught in a very watered-down way. While they are lovely tools, their true potential is often missed. The usual approach relies on consistency and belief. We write an affirmation, repeat it over and over, perhaps visualise or feel it, and assume that this is enough. But in reality, the power of an affirmation does not come from repetition alone.

The strength lies in the words you choose, and in how you consciously move the energy in a positive direction. Rather than just saying an affirmation, we can activate the consciousness within us. This is far more powerful. You're not just speaking words; you're commanding energy to move. It comes from a place of authority, rather than hope.

In fact, when an affirmation is properly activated, you only need to say it once. When it is done in the correct way, incorporating conscious energy movement in a positive direction, it holds far more power than repeating it endlessly.

Another key factor in amplifying the power of any affirmation is how you say it. Most people start affirmations with *I* or *I am*, because that's how we naturally refer to ourselves. But the subconscious mind doesn't respond to *I*; it responds to *you*.

By addressing your subconscious and your soul directly, you activate the part of yourself that truly creates change.

So, instead of saying:

I am confident,

You would say:

You are confident.

This small but profound shift speaks directly to your subconscious mind and sends the energy where it can create real transformation.

When you align your words with intention, authority, and energy, affirmations become more than just a repeated statement, they become a powerful activation of your own inner consciousness, capable of shifting frequencies and creating results far faster than just repetition alone ever could.

Subconscious Affirmation Activation Exercise

Take a deep breath and repeat the following affirmation activation silently in your mind or out loud for extra impact:

Subconscious mind, remove any lower frequencies of hurt, sorrow or disappointment and download the frequency that you are pure love and nothing can get in the way of that or take that away from you.

You will feel lighter as the energy shifts. You might find that you yawn, shudder or even burp as you move the stagnant energies. This is just your body's way of releasing stagnation or slow moving energy. Yawning stretches your energetic system to receive more flow. Shuddering allows the body to remove trauma and lets the frequencies adjust to clear the energy, and burping releases negative gases that have built up and are not needed.

As I mentioned in previous activations, if you feel any resistance then just ask spirit to remove the resistant spirit from you and send it over to the light, then redo the activation.

Affirmation Exercises Using the Power of You

Affirmation activations are incredibly powerful in moving your reality forward in a positive way. Below are a few examples you can start using:

Affirmation 1 - *To Remove Fear*
Soul, the fear of the unknown is leaving your body right now and you are remembering that there is no fear of the unknown within you. You are fearless and unstoppable. Everything is moving in the right direction for you. Subconscious mind, download that truth into my body as it is right now.

Affirmation 2 - Moving in a Positive Mindset
Subconscious mind, you love all the good that life has for you and you love all the good that is coming into your life today. Subconscious mind, download that as the truth into my reality as it is right now and remove anything in the way of that new reality.

Affirmation 3 - A Positive Day Ahead
Subconscious mind, today is going to be the greatest day of your life. You are exactly where you are meant to be. Your frequency

is so high that you are unstoppable. You feel so happy today. Subconscious mind, download that as truth in my reality as it is right now.

Affirmation 4 - Acknowledging Self-Love
Soul, you are blazing yourself with pure love right now and acknowledging how loved you are. Activate and begin! Thank you God! It is done!

Affirmation 5 - Good Experiences
Soul, infuse exciting energies into your body right now that something good is going to happen to me today! Activate and begin! Thank you God/Spirit, I say yes to this. It is done!

Why not try writing your own powerful affirmation activations to bring into your daily practice and see how your life begins transforming?

There is some space below for you to create and write your own personal, powerful activation affirmations, or you can use your own notebook to write them in.

1. ____

____

____

____

____

____

____

____

____

2. ______________________________

3. ______________________________

4. ______________________________

Chapter 4 – The Effects of Childhood Trauma

There's no handbook for life and all of the twists and turns that come with it. Navigating everyday challenges isn't always easy. Being an adult can be complicated, and when we add trauma from childhood experiences into the mix, it's a recipe for even more complications and a very undesirable outcome.

Unless we have had a severely traumatic childhood, most of us don't think about our younger years every single day. Happy or sad memories might pop up here and there, but we often dismiss the niggles from childhood. It's not usually something we reflect on daily, until something triggers us. Suddenly, we're catapulted back to our childhood, and in that moment all the memories come flooding back. We realise that we've never actually overcome certain experiences or traumas, and that they've impacted us on a much bigger scale than we imagined.

As humans, we often push these memories away, burying them deep in our subconscious. Then, when they resurface, it can feel as though we're drowning in deep water, not knowing if we will sink or swim. We're left trying to survive the resurfacing feelings we thought had been long forgotten.

These emotional experiences creep up on us in adulthood from seemingly nowhere, like a huge tidal wave. That is when we realise we are not healed at all, and that these traumas have been tightly stored within our unconscious and subconscious mind, waiting for the right moment to rear their head.

Our brain is similar to an aeroplane's black box. An aircraft stores all its information in a black box that records every detail of the flight. In the same way, our mind and energy system store all of the information from every timeline of our existence into our own human *black box* within the subconscious. Its capacity is almost unlimited.

The motivational speaker Brian Tracy states that by the age of twenty-one, you've already permanently stored more than 100 times the contents of the entire *Encyclopaedia Britannica*. The human mind is incredibly powerful, but it can also impact us in a detrimental way if much of what is stored in our black box is negative. This is why understanding our past experiences, and the way our thoughts affect us, is crucial if we want to heal and create more positive thought processes and memories.

I had an incredibly difficult time as a young child. When I first started primary school, there was a little girl in my class who had mental health issues, although this was not recognised or addressed at the time. Looking at it now from a spiritual perspective, I can see that as well as neurodivergent challenges and other difficulties within her human psyche, she had a disconnection from source, and an imbalance in her left and right brain hemispheres, and spiritual attachments that needed clearing.

As a little girl I didn't understand what was happening. I experienced this child throwing chairs at me, grabbing my arms and leaving nail marks, pulling huge clumps of my hair, and even urinating on me. On one occasion she threw a stick at me, narrowly missing my eye. The teachers couldn't control her and the dinner ladies didn't do anything to help. I felt lost, unsafe and unsupported.

Most days, my five-year-old self was just relieved to make it home from school in one piece and back to a safe environment. My body lived in a constant state of fight or flight, which not only impacted my emotional state but as I got older, it made me wary of others, closed off to affection, and weakened my immune system. At the time, my parents probably wouldn't have linked my teenage and early-adult health struggles to this trauma, but from all my years of study, I now know without question that these experiences were fundamental to many of my health problems.

A study conducted by the London Clinic of Nutrition found that people who experienced challenges in childhood, especially adverse ones, are far more likely to develop health issues later in life.

Looking back as painful as those experiences were, I honestly don't think I'd be here writing this book, or caring so deeply about helping both young people and adults, if I hadn't lived through them myself.

My parents did take me out of school for a short time until the girl was removed, but years later I heard that she had been sectioned as an adult. I remember once, while working in publishing in London in my twenties, thinking I saw her across the road. I had a huge panic attack and ran from my office building.

Until that day, I thought I'd moved on. I had pushed the memories down and assumed I was okay. But clearly, I wasn't. Years before, she had sent me a Christmas card, no doubt her mother's attempt at an apology for the disruption and trauma, but I couldn't even bring myself to open it. I was still too raw.

It was around then that I realised just how important it is to heal past experiences if we want to be happy and free ourselves from the walls we subconsciously build. I need to accept what happened and forgive, not just her, but also those who stood by and did nothing. Because I had felt completely alone and unsafe in that environment.

It wasn't until I began training as a healer that I truly understood how to release this dysfunctional thinking and slow-moving traumatic energy. Over time, I began to feel much calmer about those experiences.

Now, I can say that I accept what happened. In some ways, I even understand why it happened, because without it, I wouldn't have developed the empathy or become the healer I am today. When I do sessions with adults who carry childhood trauma, I can relate to and understand their pain on a much deeper level.

I've met counsellors who meant well, yet lacked first-hand experience of trauma. I never felt I could relate to them. How can someone fully understand what another human has been through if they have never experienced anything similar?

I'll never forget seeing a counsellor for issues around affection. Her advice was: 'You don't need men!' It wasn't quite the guidance I was looking for. Instead, it left me feeling even more confused and let down. I walked away feeling disappointed and not wanting to return. She simply couldn't relate to what I had been through.

Looking back at my primary school experience, I often wish I had had the knowledge and tools then that I have now. Perhaps I could have helped the girl, because she clearly held so much pain and dysfunction within her.

I am deeply passionate about helping young people with behavioural and emotional issues now, because I know firsthand how hard it is to be a child who doesn't understand what's happening to them, or how to make it stop.

I later heard that my primary school teacher suffered a nervous breakdown as a result of the trauma of teaching this girl. I don't think she ever went back to teaching again, which saddened me greatly.

Over the years, I've worked with many clients suffering from health and emotional issues rooted in childhood trauma. They often experience panic attacks, insomnia, anxiety in crowded places, and a constant fear of others.

I also liaise with parents, both of children who struggle with behavioural and mental health issues, and of children who are victims of trauma or bullying. By working on the root causes of emotional triggers and trauma, I've seen remarkable improvements happen very quickly.

For example, I did sessions with a six-year-old boy who had terrible nightmares, fear of sleeping, and difficulty forming close emotional bonds. When I connected with his energy, I discovered that the trauma stemmed from when he was just four years old and his parents went through a messy divorce. He was holding on to the lack of connection between them and was terrified of abandonment. His mother later confirmed that my findings were correct.

After I helped to move the energy of this trauma, he began sleeping peacefully, became less anxious, and opened up more socially. He was able to trust again.

Do We Forget Past Trauma in Our Early Years?

Most of us assume that very young children don't remember trauma. Scientifically, it is often believed that a child's memory is not fully developed in the early years. Many people say things like 'Children are resilient, they won't remember that,' or 'They'll forget about it.' But research has shown otherwise.

Studies published in:

- P. J. Bauer's *Children Remember Childhood: Implications for Childhood Amnesia*
- Emily Sutcliffe Cleveland and E. Reese's *Children Remember Early Childhood: Long-Term Recall Across the Offset of Childhood Amnesia*
- K. Tustin and H. Hayne's *Defining the Boundary: Age-Related Changes in Childhood Amnesia*

all demonstrate that children can remember events from before the age of three.

From my own experiences with many young children, I have seen firsthand that trauma leaves an imprint, even when it is not consciously remembered. The subconscious and the energetic field still carry the memory. Even if a child cannot explain or recall what happened, their energy knows something is not right.

This energetic imbalance often shows up as:

- Behavioural issues
- Confidence struggles
- Sleep disturbances
- Relationship difficulties

Parents or carers often contact me when their child is struggling in one of these areas. What I intuitively sense within the child's energy field almost always matches the parent's or carer's description of events. In some cases, they are aware of the trauma, but in other cases, they have no idea. I may trace the issue to something that happened at school, or even to experiences within the womb or past-life timelines.

This is why trauma cannot always be healed by simply talking about it. Trauma is stored in the body and in the energy field.

Talking may bring relief, but the energetic imprint remains until it is released on a deeper level.

Children are especially vulnerable. If trauma is not addressed, it can alter their wellbeing and happiness well into adulthood. I see this constantly in my healing sessions, not only in children, but in adults who are still carrying unhealed wounds from their past.

Trauma also affects the ancestral line. If we do not heal it, it often gets passed down energetically to future generations. For example, if a mother struggles with alcoholism and never heals her wounds, her child is at risk of repeating that same pattern. It becomes like a hamster wheel that continues until someone chooses to break it.

I know this from personal experience. At around the age of nine, I began to suffer from extreme fears that I believe stemmed from the traumatic experiences with the girl at school when I was just five years old. I couldn't sleep in the dark or with my bedroom door closed. These fears escalated to the point where I had to share a room with my siblings or my parents because I was terrified of being alone. I carried a constant fear of being attacked, replaying incidents in my head over and over.

Eventually, I saw a psychiatrist, and while talking helped, I wouldn't say I truly healed until I began spiritual healing. Those fears had embedded themselves deep within both my subconscious and conscious mind. They lay dormant for years, stored in my energy field, until I moved the energy and cut the energetic cords to heal the root causes.

This is why I believe that while talking about your problems is valuable, as the saying goes, 'a problem shared is a problem halved'. It is often not enough for deep-rooted trauma. The slow-moving energy of trauma must be transmuted into a more positive form for true healing to occur.

In my healing experiences, I have helped both children and adults who have never even spoken to me directly. Often, it is a parent, carer, or partner who reaches out for help, and the client themselves has no idea that the healing is taking place. Yet they still benefit, because I connect energetically to their soul and subconscious mind. On a soul level, they agree to the healing, even without conscious awareness, and profound shifts take place.

Chapter 5 – Ancestral Patterns, Energetic Cords, and Family Timelines

It's not unusual for teenagers with depression to have family members who also struggle with depression, or for young adults with addiction to come from families where addictive behaviours are present. We don't just inherit DNA; we inherit energetic patterns. The emotional and behavioural traits of our ancestors can ripple through timelines and show up in our lives now.

These energetic links, often called cords, connect us to people, events and experiences from the past. They carry emotional and energetic information that influences how we react, feel, and make choices. We might think we only inherit physical traits like eye colour or height, but we can also inherit mental and emotional patterns: beliefs, fears, survival strategies and unresolved pain. If an ancestor suffered trauma, hardship or deeply held fear, that energy can lodge in the family line and continue to affect the family line until someone clears it.

Because these patterns are often unconscious, we might not know why we respond in certain ways. A family that has put their career over connection can leave later generations feeling compelled to choose career success at the cost of relationship health. A lineage immersed in lack and poverty can hand down a fear of not having enough. If left, these energetic patterns show up as anxiety, depression, addiction, relationship struggles or even physical illness.

Not all cords are negative. Some ancestral ties can bring gifts of resilience, artistic talent, healing abilities, courage and strength. I embrace the positive cords I've inherited as these are blessings that I would never want to cut away. But others have carried dysfunction, anger, shame and self-sabotage. I have spent time clearing those cords and I'm still continuing to clear cords from my lineage, so that my children have a smoother energetic path.

When negative patterns persist, they tend to repeat generation after generation, until someone chooses to break the cycle. That's why it's so important to energetically clear timelines and send unhelpful frequencies back to their origin in spirit, to transform them and release their hold. Doing this not only frees the individual, it lightens the ancestral line for everyone that follows.

I see this in my clients again and again, an unresolved pattern in a grandparent or parent showing up as mental health struggles or compulsive behaviours in a child. The earlier we notice and heal these repetitive problems, the better chance we have of stopping the chain before it affects the future generations.

Trauma from the Womb and Birth

We go about our daily lives rarely thinking about how much we impact others energetically, and yet we couldn't be further from the truth. Most people are warned about obvious physical risks during pregnancy (smoking, diet, medications), but very few are taught that emotional states, unresolved trauma, fear, or addictions, during pregnancy can also influence the unborn child's energy field. If the maternal or paternal experience during pregnancy contains high levels of stress, negativity or unresolved pain, those energetic imprints can follow the child into their life.

There have been centuries of debate about exactly when the soul enters the body after conception. My own intuitive experience is that the soul first *announces* itself through interaction, for example when the mother feels a first kick, or the baby responds to a hand on the womb. At that moment the soul is engaging and making its presence known. Sometimes the soul will float in and out of the womb as it remains connected to higher dimensions, and at other times it will settle fully into the chosen biological *spacesuit* for the duration of the human experience but either way, it will have felt the surrounding energies of its environment.

I often speak to clients who I know have been impacted energetically from when they were in the mother's womb.

Birth and pregnancy experiences can leave energetic impressions that affect both parents and baby. I've seen many cases where trauma related to conception, pregnancy or birth was held in the parent's subconscious and energy field and later showed up in the child's life as emotional, behavioural or physical challenges.

When a mother experiences prolonged stress or trauma during pregnancy, biochemical changes (such as elevated stress hormones) can influence the developing baby's brain and nervous system. Energetically, the baby is also highly sensitive to the mother's emotional state. Chronic prenatal stress may make the child more susceptible to heightened fight-or-flight responses, difficulties with emotional regulation, sleep problems, anxiety, attachment challenges and, in some cases, later physical health issues.

Unresolved trauma from the mother's past, grief, abuse, fear or loss, can be carried into pregnancy and subtly influence the baby's energy. I have seen this show up as pre-birth trauma as the child's energetic field holds an imprint from experiences that occurred while in the womb. Often neither parent remembers or recognises this, so the child and family can feel out of balance without understanding why.

If a mother was emotionally distant during pregnancy, perhaps because of her own trauma, overwhelming stress, or health complications, the baby's early attachment and development can be affected after birth. Early bonding is crucial for emotional regulation; disruptions or stress during pregnancy and the early months can make forming secure attachments harder for the child later on. Over time, those early imprints can manifest as trust issues, difficulty managing emotions, relationship struggles, and even chronic health concerns.

We don't usually have conscious memories of pre-birth experiences, and if we did, many people would never speak to their parents about these events. That's why so many people come to me with a sense of something *out of alignment*. They feel an energetic residue but can't locate the cause. In those cases I instinctively tune into the client's subconscious and energetic field to locate and move the trauma.

I also often see patterns among women experiencing fertility challenges. One client had been trying to conceive a second child for over two years with no medical explanation. When I tuned into her energy, I immediately saw an unresolved traumatic birth from four years earlier, which led to an emergency caesarean and a blood transfusion. She had never realised that this birthing experience was still energetically active and was impacting her ability to conceive again.

We moved energy to release the fear, the shock and the embedded trauma at a subconscious level and reprogrammed the limiting beliefs that had been holding her back. After two focused energetic sessions she felt a huge internal shift. Within eight weeks she conceived and later gave birth to a healthy baby. I share this as an example of how powerful pre and perinatal energy can be, and how clearing it can sometimes produce rapid, life-changing results. *(Every case is unique; I do not promise the same outcome for everyone.)*

When I clear womb and pre-birth trauma, I will tune into the client's energetic field to locate imprints from conception, pregnancy, birth, or ancestral timelines. I then release emotional energies associated with the trauma and transmute slow-moving energy into a high vibration. I reconnect and soothe the client's inner child and pre-birth self, holding a safe container for the wounded parts to heal. Then I reprogramme the subconscious files that maintain fear-based patterns, replacing them with safe, supportive templates, and finally seal and strengthen the energy field so that new, healthier patterns can form.

Final Thoughts

Womb and prenatal trauma can influence and shape a person's emotional and physical life and wellbeing in a profound way, long after birth.

Because it is often hidden below conscious memory, it frequently goes unaddressed, until the right kind of energetic healing reveals it and clears the way for transformation. With awareness, compassion and healing, the effects of pre-birth trauma can be released, creating a healthier, more balanced future for the child or adult and the whole lineage.

The Power of Past Lives in Healing

Many clients come to me with physical, emotional, or mental struggles that seem to have no explanation. Doctors can't find answers, tests show nothing unusual, and the client feels stuck in a cycle of frustration. They ask me: 'Why am I experiencing this when nothing in my life explains it?'

The answer often lies beyond this lifetime. We are more than our bodies, we are energy. As eternal beings, we carry energetic cords and patterns from lifetime to lifetime. If trauma from a past life remains unresolved, it leaves an imprint in our energy field and continues to influence us in the present day.

Understanding Energy and the Aura

Every human being has a physical body. This is our temporary vehicle on Earth, and an energy field, often called the aura. This aura reflects our emotional, mental, and spiritual states. When we experience joy, stress, or trauma, these experiences can leave imprints in the aura. Some fade away, but others linger, shaping our behaviours, fears, and even our health in ways we don't always understand.

If trauma has not been healed in a past life, the energy may carry forward into this one. That's why some people experience deep fears, phobias, or emotional struggles without any obvious cause.

Exploring Reincarnation

Not everyone believes in the idea of past lives. It isn't taught in our education systems, and many cultures overlook it entirely. Yet millions of people around the world do quietly hold the belief that we have more than one lifetime.

- In the United States, a 2021 Pew Research Center survey found that about 33% of adults believe in reincarnation, with younger adults under 50 more likely (38%) than those over 50 (27%).
- In Europe, belief varies between 20–25%, with countries like Lithuania reaching as high as 44%. In contrast, East Germany shows only 12%.
- In Canada, a 2010 survey found that 27% of adults believe in reincarnation.

While these numbers may seem small, they show that reincarnation is a concept that resonates across cultures. Personally, I believe understanding past lives is essential if we truly want to understand ourselves, our emotions, and our purpose here on Earth.

How Past Lives Shape the Present Day

Our soul experiences many lifetimes, playing different roles, facing joys and challenges, and always learning. These experiences leave energetic imprints that can influence us in the following ways:

- Unresolved trauma can show up as phobias, anxiety, or emotional blocks.
- Patterns of behaviour may repeat, such as victimhood, self-sabotage, or fear of success.
- Talents and gifts may carry forward, giving someone natural healing abilities, artistic skill, or wisdom they cannot explain.

Books like *The Power of Past Life Regression* by Steve Burgess and *Journey of Souls* by Dr. Michael Newton, both contain countless stories where there is evidence that past life memories exist.

I have included below, several case study examples from my own healing sessions with clients. These cases relate to past life experiences that had significantly influenced the clients present day lives.

CASE STUDY: *Fear of Fire*
One mother brought her four-year-old son to me because he had an extreme fear of fire. Even hearing the word would terrify him. When I tuned into his energy, I saw a past life in the 1900s where he had died in a high-rise building fire. The memory was still imprinted in his energy field.

By clearing that imprint, his subconscious was released from the fear, and the change in him was remarkable. Without addressing the past life root, this phobia could have intensified as he grew older.

CASE STUDY: Fear of Losing Family
Another case involved a 15-year-old boy who suddenly developed severe anxiety about losing his mother. Through healing sessions, I uncovered a past life where he had been separated from his family. His subconscious reactivated this fear when he reached the same age he had been in that past life trauma. After clearing the energy, his anxiety lifted, and he was able to move forward without the constant fear of abandonment.

CASE STUDY: The Impact of Abuse
In one session, I saw that a client had been in an abusive relationship in a past life. She carried this unresolved pain into her present reality, where it manifested as deep distrust in relationships. Once we cleared the energetic imprint, her perspective transformed. She could approach relationships with openness instead of fear.

Soul Contracts and Familiar Connections

Before we are born, we often make soul contracts, agreements with other souls to experience certain lessons together. This is why we sometimes meet someone and instantly feel we've known them forever, or why a place feels strangely like home. These connections often come from past lives and unfinished contracts.

Patterns and Physical Issues Related to Past Lives

Past life trauma doesn't always show up as fear. It can also influence behaviours, habits, and even physical symptoms. Below are some examples of this:

- Success and Failure: Someone who lost everything in a past life may fear risk-taking now, playing it safe and doubting their worth.
- Food and Starvation: Past lives of famine or deprivation can manifest as eating disorders or unusual food habits.
- Hair Pulling Disorders: Conditions like trichotillomania (hair pulling) sometimes have past life roots. In monasteries and convents, people were forced to pull hair as a sign of devotion or to receive food. This created patterns of guilt, shame, and compulsive behaviour that can resurface in present-day lives.

By uncovering these causes and clearing them, clients often find rapid relief where nothing else has worked.

Healing Past Life Energy

When focusing on healing past life issues, it's not always helpful for the client to fully relive those past life experiences. In traditional past life regression sessions, clients may often go back in time to visually experience traumatic memories which can sometimes feel overwhelming and even unhelpful in some cases, where we are wanting the client to move into better energy. Instead, I often tune into the energy, identify the imprint, and clear it without requiring the client to know every detail of the past life. I will clear imprints from the aura and subconscious, release any guilt, anger or fear and reprogramme the subconscious with healthier patterns.

This process allows the client's soul to acknowledge the old experience, release it, and align with higher vibrational energy.

When we release past life imprints, we clear stagnant energy and free ourselves from repeating cycles. This creates space for balance, joy, and new possibilities.

In my experience, many unexplained phobias, compulsions, and emotional challenges stem not from this life, but from lives before. Once addressed, they can dissolve quickly, leaving clients free, lighter, and more empowered.

Conclusion

Our past lives are not just stories, they are energetic realities that continue to shape us until they are healed. By recognising and clearing unresolved trauma, we can transform our present life, understand our behaviours more deeply, and move closer to our true potential.

Healing past life imprints is not about dwelling on the past, it is about liberating the client's soul, so that they can move forward in peace, with happiness, purpose, and freedom.

Chapter 6 – Do Other People's Judgements Affect Us?

Have you ever felt judged so deeply that it knocked your confidence, left you feeling angry, or even made you doubt yourself? Judgement has a profound impact on us. The opinions of others, especially those formed when we are young, can leave lasting imprints that carry into adulthood.

Positive judgement can boost self-esteem and make us feel seen and valued. But negative judgement often has the opposite effect, leading to insecurity, self-doubt, anxiety, and even depression.

From our teenage years onwards, many of us begin to alter our behaviour, opinions, and appearance just to avoid criticism, bullying, or exclusion. While this helps us feel accepted, it often comes at a cost because we lose touch with our authentic selves. Over time, we may become so focused on pleasing others that we forget who we truly are.

Fear of judgement can also hold us back. It can cause hesitation when making important choices in careers, relationships, or personal expression. Some people follow socially approved paths instead of their soul's calling which leaves them unfulfilled and disconnected.

Criticism from family, teachers, peers, or social media can create stress, insecurities, and even depression. Yet not all judgement is harmful. Constructive feedback, when offered with compassion, can encourage growth and help us refine our skills. The key is balance and discerning between feedback that uplifts us and judgment that suppresses us.

When fear of judgement rules us, it can block intimacy and vulnerability in relationships. In contrast, feeling accepted and understood allows authenticity to flourish and bonds to strengthen.

A Client's Story: Clearing Subconscious Judgement

I once did a healing session with a client who felt incapable of finishing anything he started, whether a project, a hobby, or even work tasks. He came to me frustrated, seeking guidance.

As I connected with him intuitively, I could clearly see that as a child he had been constantly judged. No matter what he did, it was never good enough by his parents or his teachers. Eventually, he gave up before completing anything, believing it was pointless to try.

After our session, I shared this insight with him. He broke down in tears, feeling an immense release. For thirty-three years, he had carried those judgments within his subconscious mind and energy field. Once the imprints were cleared and reprogrammed, he began to feel lighter and more capable.

Six months later, he told me he had never felt so fulfilled in his career. For the first time, he continued with projects even when faced with challenges, because he now had the faith and determination to follow through.

Society's Judgement

We live in a world steeped in social expectation. From a very young age, children absorb the opinions of adults that are often shaped by cultural expectations, traditions, and collective beliefs. These judgements filter down into schools, peer groups, and eventually adulthood, creating a cycle that repeats without awareness.

Criticism takes many forms: disapproval of choices, appearance, lifestyle, or success. We stereotype, label, and measure worth based on wealth, academic achievement, or social status. The *matrix* of society has convinced us that perfectionism equals success, and that high academic grades guarantee a better life.

Yet not everyone is academically inclined. Many people thrive through creativity, emotional intelligence, or spiritual gifts. Sadly, the education system rarely teaches us about emotional wellbeing, energy awareness, or mental health which are all the very tools that truly sustain us in life.

When we allow society's judgements to dictate our path, we risk betraying our authentic selves. Following someone else's idea of success leads to emptiness, not fulfillment. True success lies in following what excites and inspires us. These are our natural gifts, our passions, our soul's calling.

Judgement, at its root, is never really about us. It often comes from another person's unhealed wounds or unmet needs. It is a projection of their own inner struggle. Recognising this truth frees us from carrying the weight of their opinions.

Breaking Free from Ancestral and Social Patterns

Judgement also runs through ancestral lines. Parents often project their own fears, regrets, or unfulfilled dreams onto their children, believing they are guiding them 'for the best'. But this frequently results in suppression, resentment, or misalignment on our true path.

For example, my dad chose a career in accountancy because this was a financially secure path that his parents and society guided him on. It gave him financial security, but it meant putting aside his real passions for acting and singing which he ended up doing just as a hobby. Even though he worked hard to provide for us, I believe he carried regrets about not following what he truly loved, because he had an audition at a prestigious acting school that he never pursued. Watching this taught me how limiting we can make ourselves when we don't fully align to our soul's and instead follow society's opinions.

I, too, experienced this personally. After receiving my GCSE results, I felt judged and ashamed because I hadn't achieved what was considered 'good enough' academically. My dad's disappointment left a deep mark on me. Years later, I realised this was never about my worth, but about societal conditioning. By healing this trauma, I was able to break the pattern and will now try consciously to parent my own children differently so that this pattern doesn't repeat.

When we don't address these patterns, they repeat across generations. Parents judged harshly as children may unconsciously judge their own children, creating a hamster wheel of criticism and suppression. Healing these cycles allows future generations to live with more freedom and authenticity.

Healing Judgement

To live freely, we must heal the wounds of judgement. Resentment, anger, and insecurity trap us in low frequencies and keep us prisoners of the past.

Healing requires releasing the energetic imprints of judgement, both those directed at us and those we project onto others. Spiritual practice leaves no space for judgment. Instead, it invites compassion, understanding, and acceptance.

We must also be mindful of how easily we judge public figures, celebrities, or even strangers without truly knowing them. This behaviour may seem harmless, but it carries low vibrational energy that sustains negative patterns in our collective consciousness.

When clients come to me with relationship struggles or feelings of inadequacy, I often find they are repeating patterns from their childhood and judgements they absorbed from parents or caregivers. Healing these wounds doesn't just free the individual; it also prevents the cycle from passing to future generations.

Living Beyond Judgement

Abundance is not about money alone, it is about emotional and spiritual fulfillment. Money itself is energy, and when we live in alignment with our soul's path, we naturally attract what we need. True abundance comes from being happy, healthy, and at peace.

This is why I encourage clients to focus on what lights them up inside. When you live in alignment with your soul's calling, 'work' stops feeling like work, it becomes service, joy, and flow. I never use the word 'work' anymore.

If you feel uncertain about your path, take time to reflect. Write down the activities and passions that make you feel alive. Look for ways to weave these passions into your daily life, career, and service to others.

Remember: you were born with unique gifts for a reason. You were never meant to follow someone else's plan or live in fear of judgement. This is your journey.

Judgement, whether from society, family, or ourselves, can suppress authenticity and create deep wounds. But by healing these imprints, breaking generational cycles, and aligning with our true passions, we free ourselves to live joyfully, abundantly, and unapologetically as who we truly are.

Judgement Healing Activation

I'm sure most of us have felt judgement at some point in our lives, even if it was self-judgement.

It's important to clear judgement because it can create feelings of unworthiness, insecurity and resentment.

Below is a healing activation to clear any judgement energy whenever you feel it is needed.

Place both hands on your heart centre. Take a deep breath and repeat the following affirmation activation silently in your mind or out loud for extra impact:

I'm calling back all parts of me that have been impacted by judgement, both spoken and unspoken.
I release the energy of needing to be understood.
I release the lie that other people's opinions define me.
I release the role of trying to prove my worth.
Spirit of judgement, I no longer need you in my energy field.
I now take you to the light and bring you into the love of God.
You are worthy, you are loved, you are heard.
It is done!

Chapter 7 – Creating Successful Relationships Through Healing

How many times have you felt misunderstood in a friendship or relationship? Maybe the communication broke down, leaving you feeling disconnected or unseen.

Throughout life at different stages, I struggled with this. I wanted to be liked and loved so I could fit in, but I rarely felt a deep soul connection with people. Most of my relationships felt surface-level. Those I truly wanted to connect with seemed to be on a completely different frequency.

Looking back, I realise that my lack of self-love was at the root of it. I carried a vibration of inadequacy, believing I wasn't enough and that's exactly what I was attracting. The universe mirrored my energy back to me, sending people who didn't value my worth. I was unconsciously saying, 'I'm not enough; I don't deserve real love or true friendship,' and so that's the reality I experienced.

This is how powerful our energy is. We create our reality through our thoughts, feelings, words, and beliefs. When we walk through life thinking we're unworthy, we'll find people and experiences that confirm that belief. Our worth does not depend on anyone else's opinion, but too often, we live as if it does.

Many of my clients have experienced the same challenges and lessons through relationships. At a soul level, we choose certain lessons before coming to Earth, often through relationships. We choose to experience emotions such as pain, rejection, and loss, not to punish ourselves, but to grow. Unlike the spiritual realms, Earth offers us the raw, human experience of emotions, and this is how we evolve.

Some of these lessons also come from past lives or ancestral patterns, and others unfold through divine timing. Relationships often act as mirrors, reflecting back the parts of ourselves we most need to heal.

True healing begins when we peel back the layers of judgement, negative self-talk, and trauma, and realise that beneath it all, we really are enough. To live fully, we must unlearn what doesn't serve us and embrace what does.

So many of my clients give off the vibration of desperation or lack. Without self-love and self-respect, they attract relationships that reflect that energy.

Here's how it works: every thought, word, and emotion carries a frequency. The universe responds by matching that frequency in our external reality. If we think we're unworthy, we'll attract people and experiences that confirm it. If we shift into love, trust, and worthiness, we'll attract those frequencies instead.

We're often taught that love comes from being in a relationship. But the most important, loving relationship we will ever have is with ourselves.

When we learn to spend time alone, to face our inner world without distraction, we build self-awareness and acceptance. Even if we don't love everything we discover, we can learn to embrace ourselves fully. And once we truly appreciate who we are, we naturally attract people who value us on that same frequency.

Being alone gives us space to face every part of ourselves. The light and the shadow. The shadow isn't something to fear; it's simply your higher self in disguise, waiting to be acknowledged and healed. As we embrace both light and shadow, we become whole, and from that place, we draw in healthier, deeper relationships.

For much of my life, I avoided being alone. I would fit myself into other people's lives just to feel liked, but in the process, I lost my identity. Over time, I learned to love solitude. Now, I enjoy travelling, writing, and even going to the theatre on my own. This solitude has been one of my greatest teachers, helping me reconnect with who I really am.

Healing Past Wounds

Many people enter relationships not out of love, but out of fear of being alone. They avoid their inner noise and trauma by immersing themselves in someone else's. I've spoken to clients who have said that they have been surrounded by friends, yet still felt deeply disconnected, because they haven't faced themselves.

This is why it's so important to heal past relationship wounds. Unhealed pain from childhood, past relationships, or even past lives can keep repeating until it's acknowledged. By cutting energetic cords and clearing trauma, we free ourselves to create healthier connections.

For example, one client of mine struggled to maintain intimate relationships. When I connected with her energy, I discovered subconscious beliefs rooted in abandonment, lack, and fear. By reversing those low frequency beliefs into higher ones, such as trust, love, safety, and connection, her reality began to shift. Within months, she was in a new, loving relationship that grew from strength to strength.

Another client came to me heartbroken after her partner repeatedly left her. When I tuned in, I saw the root of the pattern in a childhood memory from when she was five years old, and rejected in the playground. That pain of abandonment followed her into adulthood, replaying in her relationships. Once we cleared the energy and reprogrammed her subconscious, everything shifted. She no longer felt desperate to have her ex back; instead, she felt strong, worthy, and ready for a healthier love.

Past Life Influences

Sometimes relationship struggles don't come from this lifetime at all, but from past lives. I've seen clients carrying imprints of betrayal, rejection, or imbalance that show up in their current relationships.

I experienced this myself. For many years, I found it difficult to accept affection. Hugs and compliments made me stiff with discomfort. When I tapped into past lives, I discovered one where I had lived as a monk, bound to celibacy. That energy carried through, making intimacy difficult in this lifetime. Once I acknowledged and healed it, my relationships transformed.

Healing Brings Freedom

When we take responsibility for our patterns and heal the relationship with ourselves, everything changes. We stop seeking love out of need and begin choosing love out of want. We no longer look for someone to complete us because we already feel complete.

As we heal our own wounds, we stop attracting partners who aren't aligned with us. We begin to value ourselves, and in turn, draw in healthier, more fulfilling relationships.

The truth is, relationships are not just about companionship. They are powerful teachers. They reflect our wounds, our patterns, and our growth. When we heal ourselves, our relationships naturally heal too.

Remember these three key things:

- You are enough.
- You are worthy of love.
- The most important relationship you'll ever have is the one with yourself.

When you believe this fully, you'll begin to attract people who reflect that truth back to you.

Remember the affirmation: **You are enough!**

You Are Enough Activation Exercise

Say out loud the following activation:

Soul, download the affirmation, you are enough, into your subconscious mind.

While saying this, tap the top of your head three times to move and activate the energy. Notice how you feel afterwards.

If you feel any resistance or fear, ask spirit to remove the resistant or fearful energy and send it to the light. Then repeat the activation.

Tip: Take three slow, deep breaths before you start and breathe gently afterwards to notice the shifts.

Relationship Healing Summary

The heart of every successful relationship lies in effective communication. When we cannot express our thoughts and feelings openly, misunderstandings build. Over time, this can create distance, resentment, and leave us feeling isolated and unseen.

Trust is another essential foundation. Betrayals, dishonesty, or unresolved traumas, whether from this life or past ones, can erode trust and create insecurity. Without trust, a relationship loses its anchors of safety and security. This is why healing old wounds, across all timelines, is so important. If we find ourselves struggling with trust, it's worth asking: Where does this come from? How can I heal it so I can move forward?

We must also examine our expectations. Often, we carry unconscious expectations into relationships, shaped by our parents, caregivers, or ancestral patterns. When these expectations aren't communicated or met, they can lead to disappointment, resentment, and even long-term emotional or physical health issues.

Our attachment styles also play a huge role. For example, an avoidant attachment style may make intimacy feel uncomfortable, while an anxious attachment style can create dependency or fear of abandonment. By recognising and healing these attachment wounds, whether from childhood, ancestral lineage, or past lives, we can free ourselves to build healthier, more balanced relationships.

Emotional regulation is equally vital. When we struggle to manage our emotions, conflicts can lead to overreactions, withdrawal, or breakdowns in connection. These patterns often run through family lines until someone chooses to break them. Healing them allows us, and future generations, to enjoy healthier bonds.

And finally, we must not overlook physical intimacy. Physical connection creates closeness, safety, and bonding. When it fades, it can leave partners feeling rejected or inadequate. Often, intimacy issues link back to childhood wounds of feeling unloved or rejected. In some cases, past life experiences, such as vows of celibacy as a monk or nun, can still influence us today. Recognising and healing these imprints allows us to reclaim intimacy in a safe, loving way.

Aligning Your Frequency to Match Relationships

Over the years, I have asked the universe to align me only with people who match my frequency, those who see and understand me, who respect the person I am today, and who love without judgment or jealousy.

What happened was remarkable. People who were no longer aligned with me began to drift away, often without me doing anything. At first, it wasn't easy, some lifelong friendships faded, and that was painful and upsetting. But I came to see this as the universe's way of showing me my worth and guiding me toward connections that truly resonated with who I had become.

Relationships, whether intimate or platonic, are some of our greatest teachers. They mirror back what we need to learn about ourselves, our boundaries, and our values. When clients come to me feeling lonely, disconnected, or unsure about the people in their lives, I remind them that these moments are part of the process. They are opportunities to grow, to value yourself more deeply, and to call in the kinds of relationships you truly desire.

If you're feeling out of alignment in your relationships or friendships, try the activation below. Ask the universe to clear what no longer serves you and to align you with those who are your true vibrational matches. You may notice people fading from your life. It might feel lonely at first, but trust that this is creating space for the right connections to enter. In time, you'll feel free, lighter, and more authentically supported.

Relationship Healing Activation

Place your hand on your heart and take a deep breath, then say silently in your mind, or out loud for more impact:

Spirit, I'm ready to release anything that no longer serves or aligns me with the truth of positive friendships and relationships.
Clear every energy of betrayal, judgement, deceit, jealousy, or gossip from my field.
Remove me from the matrix of fake connection competition and silent resentment.
Cut every cord where I allowed myself to be small in order to belong.
Dissolve every imprint where I tolerated half hearted love or masked envy.
I now activate a divine shield we only love laughter and truth can enter.
Only those souls who speak with me with love behind my back may find their way into my circle.
Spirit of discernment self-respect and loyal love anchor and surround me now.
I am magnetic to relationships and friendships that see my soul and celebrate me.
I am surrounded by souls that speak like hold vision and protect my name.
And so it is.

If you feel any resistance, ask spirit to move the fear and resistant energies from your field over to the light, and then try the activation again.

Chapter 8 – How Our Thoughts and Emotions Affect Our Mental and Physical Health

I believe that our cells are always listening to us.

When we think poorly of ourselves, our cells hear it.

When we believe we are sick, our cells hear it.

When we carry heavy emotions and never address them, our cells hear it.

But the opposite is also true. When we affirm that we are beautiful, successful, worthy of love, and healthy, our cells hear that too.

Every thought, belief, and emotion becomes part of the relationship we have with our body. Over time, these patterns shape the reality we live in. A balanced mind and a steady emotional state are not just helpful, they are the very foundation of mental and physical health.

The True Meaning of Dis-ease

The word disease can be broken down into dis-ease. It's a signal that somewhere within us, whether in the mind, body, spirit, or emotions, something is out of balance.

If we don't address this imbalance on a deeper, cellular level, it can manifest into greater physical problems which research has shown.

These issues include:

- Negative thoughts and constant worry increase stress hormones like cortisol.
- Stress and negative self-talk can trigger anxiety, depression, and low self-esteem.
- Bottled-up emotions create emotional distress, which destabilises mood.
- Chronic stress weakens the immune system, leaving us open to illness, inflammation, and disease.

Our inner world and outer health are intimately connected.

When the Soul Says 'No' and the Body Is Your Messenger

I've met people who were seriously unwell and told me they wanted to heal. Yet when I tapped into their subconscious, I received a different message: part of them was afraid of life, or simply tired of living.

In these cases, the body wasn't responding to healing because, at a soul level, they weren't ready to stay. This is why some people thrive with treatments, whether medical or holistic, while others do not.

Healing cannot be forced. It only happens when the soul chooses it.

As a healer, I never override free will. Instead, I help clients explore what their soul truly wants. When they realise they may have unconsciously resisted healing, we begin to shift that energy. From there, reprogramming the subconscious allows space for genuine change.

The body is our messenger and time and time again, I've seen clients with chronic illness or pain that had no clear medical explanation. When I tuned in energetically, I discovered the pain wasn't random, it was the body's way of communicating.

Our bodies send signals when energy is out of balance. At first, these signals may be small: fatigue, discomfort or mood swings, but if ignored, the signals grow louder, creating pain, illness, anxiety, and depression, until we can no longer avoid them.

The body does not betray us; it speaks for us when we are not listening to ourselves.

My Own Healing Journey

In my late twenties, I was very unwell. I suffered from chronic illness, fibromyalgia, and M.E. Looking back, I know these conditions were connected to deep emotional and energetic imbalances.

I was going through stress, difficult friendships, and the aftermath of a divorce. My nervous system was out of alignment. My energy was scattered and unbalanced. Even the left and right hemispheres of my brain were not working in harmony.

I realised I needed to transform the stagnant heavy energy into higher vibrations. By rebalancing the electrical, chemical, and magnetic frequencies of my body, I began to release pain and restore harmony. As my system realigned, my health gradually returned.

At that time, I was deeply unhappy in myself and in my outer world. I struggled with self-love and felt trapped in my career, unable to express my creativity and this was clearly showing up in my body, because the pressure built up inside me until my body eventually erupted.

I remember the day I lost my Nan, on the very same day, my toddler daughter had a serious fall. The emotional stress overwhelmed me, and my body responded with a painful skin rash.

My skin mirrored my inner state: angry, grief-stricken, restless, and traumatised. This was a turning point in my understanding of how closely emotions and physical health are linked.

The problem is we so often try to mask the pain. For a while, I relied on painkillers and antidepressants, but they only concealed my issues. In fact, they brought more side effects, and at one point I even fainted from the strength of the pills. My body was trying to warn me, sending signals of disruption, urging me to stop covering up the real problem.

Medication can offer relief, but if the root cause isn't addressed, then the volcano inside us will eventually erupt.

Stories of Transformation

Many of my clients suffered from chronic pain or sickness and were prescribed medication, yet tests show no clear medical cause.

The pattern was always the same: when life was calm, the pain was manageable. But when emotional stress returned, the pain flared up. It was never resolved, only suppressed.

Once these clients began spiritual healing treatments, their pain started to lift. They were able to gradually reduce, and in some cases completely come off, long-term medication. By addressing the emotional and energetic root, they rediscovered their true selves and regained their health.

When pain persists without explanation, it's a sign to look within. Subconsciously, pain is often linked to guilt, punishment, or unhealed experiences from the past.

Until we release these attachments, the body will keep carrying them. But once we understand why these experiences manifest, and reprogramme our subconscious with healthier thought patterns, the body begins to heal.

Rethinking Mental Health Issues

Today, mental health struggles are rising. Anxiety, depression, and mood disorders are seen everywhere. But I believe many of these conditions are not permanent illnesses, but emotional responses to imbalance.

The DSM-5 lists nearly 300 mental health disorders. While diagnostic labels can be helpful, they can also trap people into believing they are *broken*.

What if, instead of immediately prescribing medication, we first explored the emotional and energetic roots? What if intuitive healers were accessible alongside doctors, to help people uncover what their subconscious is really carrying?

One woman I worked with had been on antidepressants for years. When she began attending my Healing House sessions, she started exploring her energy field at a soul level. With her doctor's support, she slowly reduced her medication and, within a month, came off of it completely.

Through our sessions, she realised her depression was rooted in teenage trauma that had haunted her subconscious. Once we cleared and reprogrammed those old patterns, her healing accelerated.

Her story is proof that healing doesn't always have to come from a pill, it can come from within.

Choosing Higher Frequencies

Our emotions carry frequencies. When we sit in fear, scarcity, sadness or hopelessness, we vibrate at a lower frequency. These states can attract unhealthy patterns, negative experiences and even spiritual attachments.

That's why it's so important to redirect our thoughts and conversations.

For example, if I catch myself saying:

'I've had such a bad day, everything has gone wrong.'

I stop and redirect the energy into a higher vibration by saying:

'But the day isn't over yet. Things are already getting better. I trust that everything will work out great.'

By shifting our words, we shift our vibration, and that shift shapes our reality.

Our thoughts are like orders placed with the universe. If we keep changing our minds, the universe receives mixed signals. It's like ordering a salad in a restaurant, then changing your mind five times about what should be on it. The server eventually brings back something you didn't even want, because your order was unclear.

Healing and desires work the same way. Clarity in our thoughts, speech and actions creates clarity in our reality.

Practices That Support Mental Health

While energy healing works on the subconscious, we also need daily practices that lift us into higher frequencies. Creativity, play, time in nature, reading, open communication, movement, singing, dancing, imagination, and quality time with loved ones all strengthen mental health.

When we focus on 'joy' rather than 'poor me' energy, we move into balance.

Depression and poor mental health often stems from unexpressed anger. Anger we feel we don't have the right to have. Beneath it lies hopelessness.

Anxiety, on the other hand, is often rooted in not trusting life. It may come from trauma, from a moment we stopped feeling safe, or even from past-life or ancestral experiences that still live within us.

True healing requires us to go deeper than the surface symptoms.

In today's fast-paced world, many people avoid stillness. They distract themselves with work, technology, social media, or television, because they're afraid of what they might feel if they stopped, but it's crucial if we want to improve our mental wellness.

Healing requires us to sit with ourselves, to look at what is really happening inside. This can feel uncomfortable, even vulnerable. Yet it is in this stillness that true transformation begins.

Sometimes mental and emotional distress doesn't just come from within us, but from outside energies. Spirits, curses, and hexes can attach themselves to us, distorting our thoughts and emotions. This is why protection, cleansing, and awareness of spiritual attachments are so important (I explore this further in Chapters 16 and 17).

Our thoughts and emotions shape our health more deeply than we realise. The body, mind, and spirit are not separate, they are one. When we learn to listen, rebalance, and consciously shift our energy, we create harmony on every level.

Healing starts with the simple truth: our cells are always listening.

Chapter 9 – Healing from Grief

Grief is a deeply personal experience, and it affects everyone differently. It can appear suddenly, sometimes swallowing us whole in a matter of seconds. No two journeys through grief are the same, because we all process loss in our own way.

Sometimes, we might feel frustrated or even resentful when someone else doesn't express grief the same way we do. This is not about them, it's a signal that there's still healing needed within ourselves. Grief can leave parts of us feeling raw, vulnerable, and heavy, and if left unaddressed, it can even affect our physical health.

Many people feel awkward or guilty for crying in front of others when they feel sadness or grief. Crying is natural, healthy, and necessary. Emotions are meant to be felt, acknowledged, and expressed. Whether you're grieving a loved one, a lost opportunity, or even a failed exam, tears are a powerful release of energy.

Society often teaches us that crying is a weakness. From childhood, we may have been told we're 'too sensitive', and many of us learned to hide our tears. But being sensitive is a gift. It allows us to sense energy, emotions, and the subtle layers of reality that others might miss. Sensitivity is a form of emotional intelligence.

Being sensitive does come with challenges. If we react too strongly or avoid emotional triggers, it can feel overwhelming.

But learning to acknowledge, process, and manage emotions transforms sensitivity into a true superpower.

Grief isn't limited to losing a person. We can feel it when relationships end, friendships fade, or opportunities are lost. Every form of loss can trigger deep emotional pain.

I've experienced many forms of grief myself: losing grandparents, my father, pets, and babies during pregnancy. I've also mourned the end of relationships, friendships, and a music career I poured my heart into. Every loss brought heartache, but each taught me resilience, compassion, and a deeper understanding of healing.

What helps most is learning to release the energy attached to these losses. This includes releasing guilt, *what if* thoughts, and emotional attachments that keep us tied to the past.

Energetic Healing and Cord Cutting

Grief doesn't only affect our emotions; it creates energetic attachment cords to people, situations, and places. These cords carry old identities, emotions, and beliefs. If left unhealed, they keep us stuck in cycles of pain.

Cutting these energetic cords is an important part of healing. It doesn't mean you stop loving the person or situation. It simply allows you to release the heavy attachments and move forward lighter, while still holding love in your heart.

For miscarriage or baby loss, healing and clearing the womb's energy is crucial. Holding on to trauma or energetic attachments from past losses can affect future pregnancies. Similarly, releasing attachments to lost jobs, houses, or friendships, allows us to step into healthier, more positive experiences.

Personal Stories of Healing Through Grief

I've had sessions with clients struggling years after loss. One woman couldn't move past her father's death. She blamed herself and felt her identity was lost. Through energetic healing, we released the guilt and attachment to control. Within a week, she felt like herself again. Still grieving, but no longer trapped in emotional pain.

Another client couldn't let go of a friendship lost years before. She cried whenever she heard certain songs, unable to move on. By addressing the energetic cords and emotional patterns tied to the friendship, she was able to release the pain and reclaim her emotional freedom.

These stories show that grief, even years later, can be healed with the right tools and support. Healing doesn't erase the loss, but it transforms the weight it carries.

It's okay to have hard days, to cry, and to retreat. Grief is natural and needs to be felt. But staying in a low-vibration state for too long prevents you from enjoying life's joys.

Acknowledging grief, feeling it fully, and then releasing it is the path to emotional freedom. Working with a healer can help you clear deep sadness, release attachments, and move into acceptance. Grief from relationships, friendships, or life changes deserves attention and healing, just like grief from death.

Key Takeaways

1. **Feel your grief**. Crying is natural and healing.
2. **Honour your sensitivity**. It's a gift, not a weakness.
3. **Release attachments**. Energetic cords can keep grief alive.
4. **Seek support**. Healing with a guide or healer can help move the energy.
5. **Move forward**. Grief should be acknowledged, processed, and released so you can step into life fully.

Grief is universal, but so is the capacity to heal. By acknowledging emotions, understanding energetic attachments, and releasing what no longer serves us, we can transform pain into resilience, compassion, and inner peace.

Loss Release Activation

Take a deep breath, close your eyes, place your hand on your heart and calm your mind. Then say the following out loud or silently for extra impact:

Soul, I honour the grief you carry.
I honour the ache of what has been lost.
You do not need to hold it anymore.
Spirit of grief, I now take you to the light and bring you into the love of God.

You should feel an energy shift as the grief lifts from you. If you do not feel anything, ask Spirit to remove any fear or resistance, then repeat the activation.

Chapter 10 – Healing the Younger Generation

Healing from a young age doesn't just support personal wellbeing, it creates space to form new, positive patterns that can transform an entire ancestral lineage. By nurturing healthy habits, emotional intelligence, and self-awareness early on, we can start new family lines that carry less physical, mental, and emotional burdens. Over time, this ripple effect could reduce suffering in communities and, ultimately, across the world.

We are living in a fragile and often broken society, one that is desperately in need of healing. The unhealed wounds and limiting beliefs of older generations are being passed down, creating cycles of unresolved trauma. These patterns keep repeating themselves, generating challenges in every new generation because the underlying issues are never addressed. Today, these wounds are becoming stronger, built up over decades of past trauma, family patterns, and unresolved negative energy.

Healing the younger generation is a deep passion of mine. When we educate young people, not just about themselves, but about life, energy, and the power they carry within, they begin to see the world differently. By understanding their energy and emotions, they can break generational patterns, create healthier ancestral lines, and ultimately contribute to a happier, more harmonious Earth.

The younger generation faces many challenges. Too often, children and teens carry anger, resentment, low self-worth, depression, anxiety, and other mental health struggles. These emotions can manifest in disruptive behaviour, self-harm, or compulsive patterns. Yet many young people don't understand why they feel these intense emotions. Society and conventional education rarely teaches that everything from our thoughts and feelings, to our experiences, is energy, and influences every part of our body and mind.

A buildup of stagnant, slow-moving negative energy, combined with excessive technology use, social media, video gaming, radiation exposure, poor diet, environmental toxins, and lack of physical activity, all contribute to a decline in mental and physical wellbeing. Without awareness and guidance, children often struggle to navigate these pressures, which can limit their potential and affect the collective consciousness of future generations.

The Impact of Social Media Platforms on Youths

More sensitive souls are being born into this world, yet they often cannot cope with the harshness of technology and social media platforms. I remember hearing about a live suicide video posted on TikTok a few years ago. This video was available for anyone to watch, and anyone with access to the platform could have stumbled across it. TikTok is legally advised for users aged sixteen and above, but in reality, many younger children access it easily. If a child has a phone, they can figure out how to install these apps in very little time.

The trauma of seeing such content as an adult would be devastating, so it's easy to imagine the far greater impact on younger generations. It isn't just TikTok, videos of a negative or harmful frequency are uploaded constantly across all social media platforms. Even a brief glance can energetically embed these images and messages into a young person's subconscious.

Trolling and Cyberbullying

Bullying has always existed, but today it is amplified through technology. Children and teens are bombarded by negative words and criticism twenty-four seven, often from complete strangers. Most of us experienced playground teasing in our childhoods, but now the digital world brings relentless exposure to unkind words.

Words carry energy, yet this is rarely taught in schools. I remember working with a young client who spent hours scrolling through harsh comments about herself. The negativity infiltrated her mindset, lowering her self-worth and triggering suicidal thoughts. Her energy had absorbed these frequencies of doubt and lack, leading to constant comparison with others, separation, and emotional distress.

Through a healing session, we cleared the subconscious mindset, removed the energetic coding from the negative words, and released attachments to these limiting beliefs. I also created a protection grid around her and taught her how to use it regularly. Months later, she reported feeling happier and more content after taking a short break from social media and then only following uplifting accounts. She continued to use the protection technique and scheduled regular clearings with me to maintain her energy. (You can find the *Box Technique* in Chapter 17.)

The Illusion of Social Media Perfection

Social media often portrays only what people want others to see. Filters and carefully curated posts create false perceptions of life and self-worth. Many seek approval, presenting different versions of themselves to fit in. Celebrities amplify this issue, often showing only fragments of their lives that appear effortless and perfect.

This distorted reality promotes comparison, separation, and unrealistic expectations. In truth, everyone, celebrity or not, faces struggles. Misconceptions about others' lives are one of the most self-destructive patterns a person can adopt.

The matrix of society has also created hierarchies that make people feel inferior or lacking. But every human begins life as an equal soul. Feeling separated from others blocks the frequency of love, which cannot coexist with a frequency of lack. By focusing on what uplifts us and practicing gratitude, we create space for positive experiences and higher vibrations.

Affirmation Activations: Raising Your Vibration and Empowering Your Soul

Below are activation affirmations to help you practise positive thinking, raise your energetic frequency, and nurture a happier, more empowered self.

Noticed that each affirmation addresses your soul directly using 'you' instead of 'I'. Speaking to the Soul bypasses resistance from the ego and subconscious doubts. You are channelling guidance from your higher self to your human self, accessing your divine essence and innate wisdom.

If you are a caregiver or parent, share these powerful affirmation activations with the young people in your life so they too can begin practising these techniques and protecting their energy.

Soul, you always embrace the positives within you and give yourself a reason to feel thankful for life.
Soul, you are incredible just as you are.
Soul, you are always loved.
Soul, you are an amazing being with so much to give to this world.
Soul, you are in the exact right place at the exact right time.

It is so important to start the day in a high vibrational and positive frequency.

There is space below for you to write your own powerful affirmations, or you can use your own notebook. You could repeat these daily to increase your vibration and feel uplifted.

1. ______________________________

2. ______________________________

3. ____

____

____

____

____

____

____

____

____

4. ____

____

____

____

____

____

____

____

News and Media Influences on Health and the Younger Generation

The news and media generate an immense amount of fear and anxiety, which deeply impacts our society, our health, and our mindset. During the Covid pandemic, for example, it was clear how media exposure shaped people's reactions. Those who immersed themselves in the news often experienced higher levels of fear, stress, and anxiety, while those who limited their exposure, myself included, were able to carry on with life more calmly. My children, at the time, were largely shielded from these fears, and today my eldest, who was six, turning seven, during the pandemic, barely remembers the intensity of it.

Unfortunately, many children were heavily affected, and I still see the effects now, as parents reach out to me about mental health challenges stemming from that time. The world contains its share of obstacles and darkness, but protecting our energy and the energy of those in our care is crucial to maintaining harmony and well-being.

If we think about it, how often do we see news that inspires happiness, hope, and healing? Rarely. Negative news dominates, and it actively shapes our thoughts, emotions, and even our physical health. Watching or hearing distressing content activates multiple areas of the brain, as explained in more detail below:

- Visual cortex (occipital lobe): this is the brain's camera. It sees images, colour and movement and helps you recognise faces and places.

Example: you notice a red ball rolling across the room.

- Auditory cortex (temporal lobe): this is the brain's radio. It hears sounds, speech and background noise and helps you make sense of what you hear.

Example: you hear someone calling your name over the noise of traffic.

- Prefrontal cortex (frontal lobe): this is the brain's manager. It helps you think things through, make decisions and control your emotions.

Example: you calm yourself down instead of snapping when you are angry.

- Amygdala (deep in the temporal lobe): this is the brain's alarm system. It reacts quickly to scary or shocking things and triggers fear or panic.

Example: you jump when you hear a loud bang.

- Hippocampus (near the amygdala): this is the brain's filing cabinet for memories. It stores important or surprising events so you can remember them later.

Example: you remember a frightening event from childhood.

- Quick memory trick: **See, Hear, Think, Alarm, Remember** - that maps to Visual, Auditory, Prefrontal, Amygdala, Hippocampus.

Words, Energy, and Fear

The media thrives on darkness. Fearful content keeps society in a low-frequency, vulnerable state, making it easier to influence and control. Constant exposure to negative words, images, and stories affects our energy, aura, and even our physical well-being. Over time, it can deplete our energy, lower immunity, and create mental and emotional instability.

This energy also affects the younger generation. Even if children don't actively watch or follow the news, they absorb the energy around them, influenced by the emotions and opinions of adults. Our auras extend beyond our physical body, and energy from others, fear, anxiety, or hostility, can attach to us and linger in our living spaces.

For example, a client of mine experienced a panic attack in a busy supermarket, overwhelmed by the energy of others during Covid. After clearing her energy using simple techniques, she felt instantly lighter. This shows how profoundly our surroundings and other people's energies can influence us.

Protecting Your Energy

I have avoided mainstream news for years because it negatively impacted my mindset and energy. I also avoid negative films, negative music, and negative media because of their energetic effects. As a child, I remember watching BBC Children's *Newsround* and feeling emotionally overwhelmed by graphic images and content. Today, similar programming continues in some schools, but I believe it should be the parent's choice whether their children engage with this material.

We cannot shield children from all adversity, but limiting exposure to unnecessary negativity can protect their emotional and energetic well-being. What we think, absorb, and speak shapes our reality. Exposing children to constant fear or scaremongering can create long-term mental and emotional effects.

I studied English and Journalism at university and initially aimed to become a news journalist. Early on, I realised much of the industry prioritised sensationalism over truth, manipulating words to sell stories rather than report facts. Even before fully practicing spirituality, I understood the power of words and the energy they carry. Choosing not to follow that path allowed me to maintain integrity and avoid contributing to fear-based media that impacts human energy.

When we immerse ourselves in these lower frequencies of fear and scaremongering, it can feel overwhelming and scary but the energy we absorb can be shifted just as quickly as it is taken in. Through clearing and reprogramming subconscious energy, we can release negativity and replace it with uplifting, high-frequency experiences. Fear and stress weaken our immune system, while faith, hope, and positive energy strengthen it. Maintaining a high-frequency mindset is essential for mental, emotional, and physical well-being.

Quick Energy Release Technique

Here's a simple energy release technique to use whenever you feel overwhelmed by fear, negativity, or low-frequency energy:

1. **Clap your hands three times and say out loud:**

Spirit releases people's energy from my energetic field now.

When you do this, you may notice your body responding in different ways, maybe a shudder, a yawn, a laugh, a tear, a cough, a burp, a wave of heat or chills, or even a little shake. This is completely normal. It simply means your body is letting go, clearing, and shifting stagnant energy.

This is a simple practice, yet incredibly powerful. You can use it anytime you feel the need, and it will help you feel lighter almost immediately. We clap three times because the number three represents completeness. It helps clear energy, seal intentions, activate new possibilities, and even shift timelines.

Sometimes, you might try the technique and not feel much at all. That's okay. This often means there's some resistance energy holding on. This resistance could come from fear, unresolved emotions, or energy attachments. If that happens, simply say the following affirmation, then repeat the technique:

2. **Clap your hands three times and say out loud:**

Release the resistance and fear spirit from my four-body system and send it over to the light with love.

Note: Your four-body system is your mind, body, spirit, and soul.

Once you have done the above resistance removal, repeat the **Quick Energy Release Technique** again. Now you should feel a shift!

The Impact of Technology on Our Energy Field

Technology is evolving at such a rapid pace that it can be difficult to fully understand its impact on human behaviour, sometimes we only realise it when it's too late and has already affected our well-being. Just look around in cafes, restaurants, or public spaces: so many adults, teens, and children are absorbed in laptops, iPads, or phones, even when out socially.

I recently engaged with a parent whose eleven-year old son was experiencing serious behavioural challenges. From his energy alone, I could tell he was suffering from technology overload. His energetic system and aura were being overwhelmed, not just by the sheer amount of screen time, but also by the constant exposure to low-frequency content, images, and language that weren't uplifting or positive.

After an intense healing session, I suggested a practical approach for the parents. They limited his iPad and television time to just one hour per day, and he was not allowed to bring any devices on weekend outings or dinners. Four weeks later, the mother reported remarkable changes. The behavioural issues had greatly reduced, and she noticed a new closeness with her son. Limiting screen time created space for conversation, connection, and understanding. He shared things about his school and friends that she had never known, became more outgoing and confident, pursued creative projects, and generally displayed happier, more positive energy. What she initially assumed were pre-teen hormonal challenges turned out to be largely influenced by technology overload affecting his energy system.

We often underestimate the effect that overuse of technology has on our energetic field. On top of that, there's the impact of Electromagnetic Fields (EMFs) - invisible energy waves emitted by natural and man-made sources. EMFs are generally classified as:

- Low-frequency EMFs – power lines, household appliances, Wi-Fi
- High-frequency EMFs – mobile phones, microwaves, X-rays

The full impact of EMFs on human health is still being studied, but some potential effects are concerning. Electromagnetic Hypersensitivity (EHS), for example, can cause headaches, fatigue, dizziness, and sleep disturbances.

Research has also suggested more serious long-term risks. For example:

- Wertheimer & Leeper (1979) found a statistical link between high-current powerlines near homes and increased childhood leukemia.
- Savitz et al. (1988) found an association between magnetic field exposure and childhood cancer risk.
- The World Health Organisation classifies radiofrequency EMFs (like mobile phones) as 'possible carcinogenic'.

Beyond physical health, EMFs can affect brain health and cognitive function, with studies noting potential impacts on memory, attention, and overall brain performance. Prolonged exposure to screens and EMFs may also affect fertility, reduce sperm quality and motility, and disrupt sleep by suppressing melatonin, which is crucial for restorative rest.

Some research suggests that EMFs may cause stress in the body's cells. This can lead to tiredness, cell damage, and lower overall energy. Even if research is ongoing and results vary, it's important to be mindful of our exposure, both for ourselves and those we care about, if we want to protect our energy, health, and vitality.

Clearing Electromagnetic Fields

Technology surrounds us, and our energy fields are constantly absorbing its effects. In every healing session I undertake, I clear radiation from the body, and without fail, I notice a profound shift, no matter the client's age. Over time, exposure to electromagnetic fields, screens, and digital devices can build up within us, creating energetic congestion that affects our wellbeing.

To help you clear and restore your energy, I've created a simple yet powerful activation. This practice is designed to release harmful toxins, chemicals, and radiation from your system, leaving your energy lighter, clearer, and more vibrant. It can be used daily, whenever you feel your energy needs a reset.

Take a moment, get comfortable, and allow yourself to fully receive the benefits of this energy-shifting activation.

Clearing EMF, Chemicals, and Toxins from the Body

Take a deep breath and say the following activation silently in your mind, or out loud for more impact:

Spirit, please clear all non-beneficial chemicals, metals, lead, mercury, arsenic, ammonia, aluminium, chloride, fluoride, cadmium and toxins within this body, and clear all radiation, implants, and attachments. Bless my pineal gland with the christ light. Thank You. Amen, It is done!

Chapter 11 – The Power of Mindfulness and Meditation

Mindfulness and meditation are not practices that, as a society, we treat with the same consistency as brushing our teeth or washing our hair, but they really should be. Some schools in the UK have introduced mindfulness into their curriculum, though it isn't mandatory. I suspect this is similar in other countries, which is a shame, because these practices enhance learning, improve concentration, and boost memory retention.

Unfortunately, many adults also don't incorporate mindfulness into daily life, so young people rarely see it in daily regimes at home. As of 2021, The National Library of Medicine reported that only about 16% of adults in Britain had learned mindfulness meditation, roughly 8.3 million adults out of 52 million. This is only a slight increase from 2018, when 15% had learned the practice. While mindfulness is growing slowly, most people still don't practice it regularly, despite its many benefits.

The Benefits of Mindfulness and Meditation

1. Mental Health Benefits

- Reduces Stress & Anxiety: Calms the nervous system and lowers cortisol (the stress hormone).
- Improves Focus & Concentration: Strengthens attention and cognitive function.

- Supports Emotional Regulation: Helps you become more aware of your thoughts and emotions, reducing impulsive reactions.
- Enhances Mental Clarity & Decision-Making: Clears the mind, supporting problem-solving and creativity.

2. Emotional & Social Benefits

- Enhances Self-Awareness: Helps you understand your emotions and reactions.
- Boosts Compassion & Empathy: Encourages kindness toward yourself and others.
- Reduces Negative Thinking: Breaks cycles of rumination and self-criticism.

3. Physical Health Benefits

- Lowers Blood Pressure & Heart Rate: Promotes relaxation and cardiovascular health.
- Improves Sleep Quality: Reduces insomnia for deeper rest.
- Boosts Immunity & Reduces Inflammation: Helps the body fight illness more effectively.

4. Benefits in Schools & Workplaces

- Enhances Learning & Memory: Improves concentration and retention for students and professionals.
- Reduces Burnout: Helps manage stress and prevents emotional exhaustion.
- Promotes a Positive Environment: Encourages mindfulness-based communication and conflict resolution.

5. Long-Term Well-Being

- Encourages a Balanced Life: Regular practice creates peace and purpose.

- Supports Personal Growth: Helps navigate challenges with resilience.

If mindfulness and meditation were integrated from a young age, especially within schools, we could see a profound shift in human mindset. Reflecting, meditating, and addressing emotions regularly allows individuals to understand their triggers and bring themselves into harmony and clarity.

Even simple changes, like replacing school detentions with mindfulness and reflection, could have dramatic effects. Detention often forces children to bottle up their emotions instead of expressing them, which stops real reflection from happening. When children are heard and understood, they are more likely to process and heal underlying triggers that cause misbehaviour.

Mindfulness and meditation give us the opportunity to be still, reflect, and observe parts of ourselves we may have ignored. Children's behavioural issues often stem from unaddressed emotional or mental stress. Adults, too, rarely understand their own energy or how it interacts with others, leading to overwhelm and imbalance. Life moves fast, and society teaches us to focus on constant doing, rather than being still and reflecting.

If we look at nature, we see that growth has seasons, Spring, Summer, Autumn, and Winter. Winter brings stillness, a sacred pause before the new cycle of growth begins. Yet humans are conditioned to push constantly, measuring success by productivity. This constant rush depletes our energy and magnetic frequencies, affecting our immunity and overall health. Slowing down, reflecting, and meditating aligns us more naturally with our bodies, helping children and adults alike to listen, heal, and grow.

Many of my clients struggle with self-love and confidence because their minds are overwhelmed by constant comparison, social media pressures, and thinking too far into the future. Alongside healing, mindfulness and meditation create space to reset the mind. Even five minutes a day, sitting, standing, walking, or cleaning, can make a huge difference over time. It's about finding your way back to the present moment, using your breath as your guide.

Practical Tips for Daily Mindfulness and Meditation

1. Start Small: Begin with 3–5 minutes daily and gradually increase.
2. Set a Routine: Practise at the same time each day, like morning or bedtime.
3. Create a Conducive Space: A quiet corner is enough; it doesn't need to be elaborate.
4. Eliminate Distractions: Turn off your phone or set it to 'Do Not Disturb'.
5. Use Guided Meditations: Apps like Headspace, Calm, or Insight Timer, and free online videos can help.
6. Practice Mindful Breathing: Focus on inhaling through the nose and exhaling through the mouth. Count breaths if helpful.
7. Incorporate Mindfulness into Daily Activities: Practise mindful eating, walking, or chores by focusing on sensations and movements.
8. Set Reminders: Use alarms or notifications to pause and take mindful breaths.
9. Link Practices to Existing Habits: Meditate after brushing teeth or before bed to reinforce consistency.
10. Keep a Mindfulness Journal: Note observations, feelings, and progress over time.
11. Be Patient: Minds wander; gently bring your focus back without judgment.
12. Celebrate Small Wins: Recognise that even brief moments of mindfulness are progress.

Gradually incorporating these practises helps mindfulness and meditation become a natural part of daily life, supporting long-term mental, emotional, and physical wellbeing.

Mini Meditation Exercises

Here are some simple meditation exercises you can try. Each has its own focus and benefits. You can adapt them for children if you like.

1. Mindful Breathing Meditation

Time: *Start with 5 minutes and gradually increase.*

Instructions:

1. Sit or lie down in a comfortable position with your spine straight so energy can flow easily.
2. Close your eyes and **focus on the feeling of your breath** entering and leaving your nostrils.
3. **Take a few deep breaths in through your nose and out through your mouth.**
4. Let your breathing settle into a natural rhythm.
5. **Notice the rise and fall of your chest or tummy.**
6. If your mind wanders, gently bring your focus back to your breath **without judgment**.

2. Body Scan Meditation

Time: *10–20 minutes, depending on your availability.*

Instructions:

1. Sit or lie down comfortably with your spine straight.
2. Slowly focus on different parts of your body, starting at your toes and moving upward (**shins, knees, thighs, etc.**).
3. Notice sensations like **warmth, tension, or relaxation** without trying to change them.

4. Spend about a minute on each body part before moving on.
5. If your mind drifts, gently return to the **body part** you were focusing on.

3. Loving Kindness Meditation

Time: *Start with 5–10 minutes and increase gradually.*

Instructions:

1. Sit or lie down comfortably with your spine straight.
2. **Start by sending warmth and kindness to yourself.**
3. Silently repeat phrases like:

- *Soul, you are happy.*
- *Soul, you are loved.*
- *Soul, you are healthy.*
- *Soul, you are living with ease.*

4. **After a few minutes, extend these wishes to loved ones, acquaintances, and eventually all beings.**
5. Imagine sending love through **colours like pink**, or any colours that feel loving to you.
6. Stay focused on the **phrases** and **feelings of compassion** until you feel immersed in love and kindness.

4. Guided Visualisation Meditation

Time: *5–20 minutes, depending on the guide.*

Instructions:

1. Sit or lie down in a quiet, comfortable space with your spine straight.
2. Listen to a **guided meditation** or imagine a **peaceful scene** in your mind (beach, forest, mountain, etc.).
3. **Notice details: warmth of the sun, sounds of waves or birds, scents around you.**
4. If your mind wanders, gently return to your **visualisation**.

5. Movement Meditation (Walking Meditation)

Time: *5–10 minutes to start, then gradually increase.*

Instructions:

1. **Find a quiet space to walk slowly and undisturbed.**
2. Walk at a slow pace, noticing **sensations of movement**.
3. **Feel your feet touching the ground and the rhythm of your steps.**
4. **Notice movement in your legs and the power in your body.**
5. Sync your **breath with your steps** if it feels natural.
6. If your mind wanders, gently refocus on the **movement**.
7. **Visualise yourself walking toward your goals. This can make you feel motivated, focused, and excited for your day.**

Benefits: Combines movement with mindfulness, reduces stress, improves focus, and supports emotional balance.

Tips for a Successful Meditation Practice

- **Consistency:** Practice daily, even for a few minutes, to build a strong habit.
- **Space:** Find a quiet, comfortable spot without interruptions.
- **Patience:** Meditation is a practice, some days are easier than others. Gently guide yourself back if you lose focus.
- **Explore:** Try different types of meditation to see what suits you best.

Each exercise can be adapted to your schedule and preferences. Experiment and find the practice that supports your wellbeing the most.

Chapter 12 – The Power of Self-Love and How We Communicate

One of the most important parts of our healing and growth journey on earth is learning to focus on self-love. This is fundamental to our overall wellbeing.

How we perceive ourselves has a profound effect on our inner energy system, and it also shapes our external reality. Like a ripple, it influences our self-esteem, resilience, and the boundaries we create with ourselves and others. It affects the way we speak to ourselves, our authenticity, our self-care, and even our ability to achieve goals and keep learning. It also impacts how others perceive us, how our relationships unfold, and how we handle forgiveness and acceptance.

As discussed earlier, technology, especially social media, television, and computer games, can have a damaging effect on how we see ourselves. The constant comparison, unrealistic standards, and widespread nature of online trolling can easily pull us into negative self-judgement.

When we truly recognise our worth and radiate that outwards, we begin to notice a shift. Our environment changes, people respond to us with more respect, and life experiences become more positive. Spiritually and physically, we stop tolerating what doesn't align with our values. What we think, we attract. To manifest the life we desire, we must first align with the vibration of worthiness. If we carry frequencies of lack, or unworthiness, those same experiences are drawn into our reality.

Mirror Exercise

This short exercise is excellent for being present, reflecting, and raising your frequency of self-love. The more you connect with the spirit of love and immerse yourself in uplifting vibrations that make you feel worthy, the more your subconscious begins to accept those experiences as truth. Your energy field, and even your cells, are influenced. By repeating these loving affirmations consistently, they filter into your mind, body, spirit, and emotions (the four-body system) and programme you to truly believe them.

Whenever you are in a room with a mirror, look into it and speak these affirmations aloud:

- *Soul, you are love.*
- *Soul, you accept yourself just as you are.*
- *Soul, you are amazing!*
- *Soul, you are beautiful!*
- *Soul, you are incredible!*
- *Soul, love flows to you and through you.*
- *Soul, you are loving, loved, and loveable.*
- *Soul, thank you for being you.*

I begin each phrase with 'Soul' and 'You' rather than 'I' because our subconscious doesn't always fully understand 'I'. Speaking directly to your soul gives the affirmations greater power.

As you become comfortable, you can create your own affirmations that resonate personally. Practising daily, both first thing in the morning and throughout the day, helps shift your energy, reprogramme your subconscious, and raise your vibration into frequencies of love. It really is that powerful.

At first, this practice may feel uncomfortable. Speaking into a mirror is not something society teaches, so it can feel unnatural or even overwhelming. Yet these moments of discomfort are often the most healing, they allow you to reclaim inner confidence and acknowledge your greatness. The more you repeat the practice, the easier and more natural it becomes.

This exercise is also powerful for children. Schools rarely teach self-love, even though it is one of the most important life skills. If a child says, 'I know I'm amazing!' they may be ridiculed or accused of having a 'big head'. Society often teaches that speaking positively about ourselves is strange or arrogant. Yet children and adults rarely understand the deep impact affirmations can have on energy and wellbeing. These statements should be part of everyday life.

I once did healing sessions with a client who suffered with severe cystic acne. She had tried countless medications and creams without success. In a distant healing session, I tuned into her energy and sensed deep self-love issues, rooted in school experiences where boys repeatedly told her she was ugly. These experiences had imprinted feelings of unworthiness into her subconscious and her cells. Together, we cleared the energy of lack, fear, insecurity, and rejection. I also gave her this mirror exercise.

Within a few weeks, her skin had cleared dramatically. More importantly, she reported feeling comfortable looking in a mirror and affirming her worth. Her healing was both physical and emotional. Acne can have hormonal links, but in her case, the root was energetic self-rejection. By addressing old wounds and teaching her to speak to her soul with love, her whole being began to shift.

Society often confuses confidence with arrogance. While both may appear similar, they are worlds apart. Confidence is healthy self-assurance, whereas arrogance is insecurity disguised as superiority. Many people downplay their strengths or put themselves down in order to fit in or to avoid judgement. Affirmations help normalise self-love. Imagine if speaking kindly about ourselves were as accepted as criticising ourselves, society would look very different.

If children were raised to see confidence as natural, they would grow into adults who are less judgemental of themselves and others. This would ripple into fewer bullying behaviours, both in schools and online. At its root, most bullies are wounded souls projecting their own pain. Teaching self-love transforms not just individuals but also the collective, creating environments filled with kindness, respect, and understanding.

Words are Energy, Words are Powerful

I'll never forget when my eldest daughter was about six years old. She came home from school and told me that her friend had said she was too slow and not very good at running. I could sense immediately from her energy that this comment had affected her. Those judgemental words were now imprinted in her subconscious mind and her energy field.

I reassured her straight away, telling her not to worry about what others say. I praised her for always trying and doing her best. I explained that we all have different strengths, and that it's perfectly natural not to be amazing at everything. The important thing is that we try, because the more we practise and believe in ourselves, the better we become. I also pointed out that, while it's never good to judge others, her friend might not realise that she actually has her own strengths in areas like art or drama. She smiled, carried on with what she was doing, and seemed settled again.

Yet I knew that the small comment from her friend could remain imprinted in her subconscious mind and energy field unless it was shifted and cleared. Outwardly, she appeared fine after my reassurance, but the subconscious can hold onto these energetic imprints long-term.

The subconscious mind is like a vast database, storing memories, experiences, habits, and emotions. These shape our thoughts, behaviours, and reactions, even though we are not always consciously aware of them. As I've mentioned earlier in this book, around 95% of our thoughts are unconscious or subconscious. Psychology and neuroscience research supports this. What it means in practice is that we can find ourselves stuck in the same unhelpful patterns, without realising we are replaying beliefs formed long ago. Even experiences from early childhood can influence us as adults.

I often hear people say that children are resilient, that they don't remember things, and that they simply 'get over it'. In my view, this couldn't be further from the truth. Many of my clients with trauma recall incidents from as young as three years old. My daughter, for example, might one day be running for a bus or cheering her child on at a school sports day, and suddenly the memory of being told she was slow could surface. Sometimes it wouldn't even return as a clear memory, but rather as an old energetic imprint of self-consciousness, insecurity, or the sense of not being good enough. Without conscious healing, those imprints remain within us and can be triggered at any point in life.

This is why it is so important to be mindful of what we say, especially to children. Our words have lasting effects.

When we criticise those around us, they don't stop loving us, they stop loving themselves. The same happens when we criticise ourselves. Every act of self-awareness makes a difference, not only to our own wellbeing but to society as a whole.

Words carry energy. They influence our happiness, our self-image, and our ability to thrive. Of course, honesty is important. But honesty can still be expressed with kindness and love, rather than judgement.

As we grow, we become increasingly shaped by society, parents, peers, and the media. Slowly we move from our natural state of openness and love into one of judgement, comparison, and criticism. Television programmes, social media, conversations at home, school or work, all feed into our subconscious and can condition us to forget who we truly are. Yet our creator intended us to live from love, not from separation or comparison.

We aren't taught that words are energy. But they are. Everything is energy, and what we hear, read, and watch shapes us more deeply than we realise. Have you noticed that the ear resembles the womb? What we listen to is conceived within us, grows, and eventually is born into our reality.

This is why it matters what we consume, not only food but also words, ideas, and media. We may be cautious about obvious negativity such as violence or horror films, but even light-hearted programmes filled with arguments, gossip, or unkindness can leave a subtle energetic imprint. I've even noticed this in children's books, where characters bully or belittle one another. These messages seep in, shaping our subconscious.

I once heard a story that illustrates this beautifully. A teacher placed two apples in a classroom. Each day, the children spoke kindly to one apple and cruelly to the other. After a week, the apple that had been treated with kindness stayed fresh, while the other became mouldy. Whether or not the story is factual, the moral remains profound: words carry power. Even if someone appears fine on the outside, harsh words can bruise the soul.

I often send prayers, loving thoughts, and visualisations to my food and water before consuming them. This helps to release any negativity they may have absorbed along the way. Interestingly, I've found that my fruit and vegetables also seem to last longer when I do this. Perhaps you might like to try it yourself.

Dr Masaru Emoto's well-known experiments with water crystals demonstrated that positive words produced beautiful crystalline structures, while negative words created distorted ones. Although his work has faced criticism, many have since repeated similar experiments with plants, rice, and fruit, with striking results. Water carries powerful codes and vibrations, and words influence those codes.

We can shift these codes not only by being mindful of what we watch and listen to, but also by consciously choosing the words we speak.

Here is a simple exercise that you can try by speaking directly to your mind:

Mind, focus on all the possibilities coming into your life today.

By speaking in this way, you align your words with truth and possibility. Directing your language creates a frequency that shifts your energetic patterns and align your subconscious with love and growth.

Humans are incredibly powerful beings. Much of our reality is created through the words we speak, to others and to ourselves.

Never forget just how powerful you are. Why not try creating your own affirmations?

Below is some space for you to write your own affirmations, or use your own notepad if you prefer.

1. ____

____

____

____

____

____

____

____

____

____

2. ____

____

____

____

____

____

____

____

____

____

3. ____

4. ____

Chapter 13 – Gratitude, Trust, and the Power of Facing Our Fears

Nobody can deny that there are times when we all want more. It's human nature.

We were born to be powerful creators, so for those who have awakened to their power, I'm sure that once the light bulb moment came, they never stopped striving for more! And although there is absolutely nothing wrong with wanting more, we also need to learn to live in an energy of contentment with what we already have, even if we don't see everything we desire immediately manifesting in our reality.

Our world has become so fast-paced that, particularly within the younger generation, there is an expectation for everything to be instant. When we are seeking to manifest something, we often don't understand that part of the process involves trusting, remaining in the vibration to receive, surrendering, and staying patient for what is to come.

I do believe that as times have changed and we have evolved, this process has become harder for younger generations. Companies like Amazon can deliver an item to our front door on the very same day, at the click of a button. We can also communicate instantly on mobiles and tablets, a long way off from the days of home telephones, phone boxes, and letters that took weeks or even months to reach their destination. Back then, we were trained to be patient because we had no choice. Patience, alongside trust, are powerful tools. Sadly, tools that we have gradually lost across the generations.

When we can truly trust and surrender, we are sending a message to the universe that we know it has our back. That all will be well, regardless of the outcome or the time it takes. This trust is powerful when we want great things to come into our lives, especially in manifesting and on our healing journey. If we can be patient and trust that our healing is working, or that what we wish to manifest is coming into fruition, then we are far more likely to see positive results. Doubt sabotages our manifesting power and lowers our frequency.

There is always a reason why we sometimes have to wait, whether it is to learn what heartache feels like, to strengthen our patience, to build resilience, perseverance, trust or determination. These are all reasons why we may not receive what we want immediately. But we must still trust that everything will work out.

Many people struggle to be patient, trusting or grateful for what they already have, and this has a huge negative impact on their external reality. Impatience, lack of trust, and not appreciating what we have all vibrate at very low frequencies. When we don't see instant results, the mind easily slips into an energy of lack. We forget to appreciate the wonderful things we already have in our lives, even the everyday blessings like a roof over our head and food on the table.

What we often don't realise is that gratitude and appreciation lift us into higher frequencies, bringing us more joy and drawing in further experiences that match those vibrations. As soon as we acknowledge and say 'yes' to the things we do like, rather than allowing negativity and lack to creep in, we open more space to create similar positive experiences in our reality. It is easy for low frequencies to creep in when we are impatient or focused on what we lack. But when we are in a frequency of gratitude, it becomes impossible for those energies to affect us.

Once we notice our blessings and truly appreciate what we have, we align ourselves with the frequencies needed to manifest more positive things, more easily and often more quickly.

Recently, I had an interactive Zoom session with a client who struggled with spending and compulsive shopping. She bought items she didn't need for a temporary high, followed by a crash that left her craving the next purchase. Together, we explored what was happening beneath the surface.

The 'buzz' wasn't about the items at all. It was the spirit of dopamine attempting to fill a deeper emotional gap, tied to lack, abandonment and disconnection from herself. Shopping gave her a temporary dose of 'I am worthy' energy, but once the hit faded, her energy dropped again. Because the inner connection to worthiness wasn't anchored, her emotions kept looping in the same pattern, trying to get her attention. Her inner self was crying out to be seen, alive and whole.

We spent some time moving the energy by clearing the feelings of disconnection, abandonment, lack and invisibility.

Before I began my healing journey, I was very similar to that client. I would often buy clothes or accessories to cover an emptiness inside me, especially when I wasn't seeing the results I wanted in my life. I believed material things would bring me contentment and joy, replacing what I felt was missing. But once I had the 'dress' or the 'shoes', the joy was fleeting. Soon I was searching for the next thing to fill the void.

Even on incredible holidays, I found it hard to feel truly happy. Instead of appreciating the moment, I was already thinking of what might bring me happiness next. What I didn't realise at the time was that I was self-sabotaging by not trusting, not surrendering, and not addressing the root cause of my discontent.

Purchasing things to escape how we feel in the present moment isn't the path to lasting happiness. It disconnects us from our soul and comes from a place of fear. Often, not knowing how to be grateful or happy creates the urge to use material items as temporary fixes.

This is very similar to deeper addictions such as drugs, alcohol, gambling or sex. Addiction is often the spirit of repetition trying to fill the space where divine presence was never allowed to be. At its root, it is a coping mechanism that begins with *'I need something to hold me'*. But what addiction is really saying is: you are deeply sensitive, your nervous system craves regulation, and your energy is waiting to be redirected.

Addiction is not weakness or failure, it is your soul saying, 'This is where I don't feel safe to be seen.' It is about recognising what part of yourself you are punishing simply for trying to survive.

When we run away from ourselves, we block the chance to understand and love ourselves. We avoid looking at the darkness, masking it with temporary highs.

I still love buying nice things and travelling to wonderful places, but I now know they are not the answer to peace and fulfilment. These days, I feel grateful for such experiences, even if other areas of my life aren't exactly where I want them to be. In the past, I couldn't have done that. I would have been too busy looking for the next 'fix' to stop and embrace the present.

Joy and appreciation come from within. It is important to understand the deep-rooted issues that prevent us from being grateful and from appreciating what we already have.

I've seen many clients whose feelings of lack stem from their upbringing, often from a parent who was consistently ungrateful or unappreciative. Some clients grew up having possessions taken away as punishment, and as adults, they now cling to items to feel safe.

Being thankful and valuing what we already have is the key to happiness. This is an aspect of ourselves that must be healed. When we go inward, acknowledge our blessings and appreciate what we already have, we discover fulfilment far greater than any material object can offer. And from that frequency, we naturally align with more wonderful experiences flowing into our lives.

It is crucial to acknowledge anything that makes us feel lacking, to understand why it is showing up, and to recognise what it is trying to tell us we need to heal.

Gratitude and Appreciation Affirmations

Practising activation affirmations for gratitude and appreciation is incredibly powerful for shifting energy and transforming mindset. Saying these affirmations upon waking, throughout the day, and just before bedtime is a simple way to start creating positive change and raising your frequency.

Remember, we have a spirit for everything. If you ever feel a lack of gratitude or appreciation, then you can ask the spirit of lack to move over into the light, and into the love of God, then call upon the spirit of gratitude and appreciation to enter your four-body system (mind, body, spirit and emotions).

When these bodies are aligned, you feel energised, grounded, and connected; when they're misaligned, you may feel stuck, tired, anxious or disconnected.

Below are some examples of activation affirmations you can start to say to incorporate into your day:

- *Spirit/God/Universe/Higher Dimensions – thank you for this wonderful day.*
- *Soul, you are filled with happiness and appreciation for everything good in your life right now.*

- *Soul, you are grateful for who you are and what you have.*
- *Soul, you are thankful for this moment and all that it offers.*
- *Soul, you appreciate that you are exactly where you are meant to be right now.*
- *Soul, you are grateful for the bed you sleep in, the roof over your head, and the food on your table.*
- *Soul, each day is a gift, and you cherish it deeply.*
- *Soul, you appreciate the small, simple moments that make life beautiful.*

I've left some space below for you to create your own gratitude and appreciation affirmations that resonate personally, or you can write them in your own notebook.

1. ____

____

____

____

____

____

____

____

____

____

____

____

____

2. ____

____

____

____

____

____

____

____

3. ____

____

____

____

____

____

____

____

4. ____

____

____

____

____

____

____

Chapter 14 – How Labels and Our Toxic Environment Are Impacting Neurodiversity

I often encounter people, particularly young souls, who have been diagnosed with varying levels of autism, ADHD, ODD, and other behavioural difficulties. As a society, we have created diagnostic labels. From a spiritual perspective, however, and through my own healing practice, I believe that while these souls may be prone to certain conditions due to genetics, the environment we now live in plays a significant role. With the abundance of heavy metals, chemicals, and toxins surrounding us, it's no wonder there has been such a sharp increase in neurodiverse diagnoses. These substances create frequency disruptions in the four-body system (mind, body, spirit, and emotions) causing dysregulation.

From my studies and experiences, I believe that many of these souls incarnate to break free from old systems that no longer hold truth. Being neurodivergent is a natural variation in how brains work. It doesn't make someone abnormal; rather, it's a sign of heightened sensitivity. Heavy metals and toxins act as disruptors, and these humans are here to challenge outdated systems, activate new pathways, and often hold more light than their environment is prepared to meet. They are special, extraordinary souls, and I often feel that the labels society assigns can overshadow their uniqueness.

Autistic individuals, for example, are often misunderstood because their frequency does not align with society's noise. They may struggle with rules and orders, not because something is wrong with them, but because they operate from a pure, original energetic template. Unlike many others, they are less affected by fear, old programming, trauma, or societal pressures. These advanced souls hold sensitive frequency grids intended to shift collective consciousness. The resistance they feel is not brokenness; it is simply that the earth matrix operates at a slower vibration than their natural calibration. Many autistic people are empaths, healers, and star beings who feel overwhelmed by the heaviness around them and haven't been given the space to fully express themselves.

Similarly, people with ADHD are not lacking focus. Spiritually, they often experience multiple frequencies at once, moving energy rapidly. This is a superpower in disguise. Their high-frequency energy cannot be confined to conventional structures. ADHD frequently emerges when the nervous system attempts to process multiple realities while creativity and intuition are suppressed. It is a signal of energy overflow, not a deficiency.

Those with ODD or behavioural challenges often embody a rebellious spirit, challenging rules and expectations to stay true to their own path. They challenge false authority and resist conforming to societal norms because they are aligned with their soul's truth. This is not defiance but a profound inner knowing. Many are warrior souls, reclaiming sovereignty when pushed into systems that lack emotional honesty or personal freedom.

Some of these souls choose these energetic experiences to transmute karma, heal ancestral lines, and teach their families about unconditional love and patience. Each individual carrying a label is undertaking a sacred assignment, always supported by the spiritual realm.

Labels can help people make sense of themselves, providing a reference point for understanding. Yet, I feel uncomfortable with over-reliance on labelling. As humans grow, develop, and evolve, they learn to navigate their difficulties. Labels, however, tend to stick, potentially limiting growth and reinforcing a fixed identity. When people see themselves primarily through the lens of a diagnosis, they may inadvertently create more limitations and struggle. From a spiritual perspective, these neurodiverse traits are gifts. Fixation on labels can prevent individuals from embracing their innate strengths, shaping their challenges into empowerment, and building confidence and self-belief.

Highly sensitive individuals, particularly those with behavioural or neurodiverse traits, often need their energy cleared regularly to maintain balance. They are perfect, unique beings here to teach society new ways of being but they do need clear energy.

We are witnessing an increase in neurodivergent children, many of whom are more sensitive than previous generations. Unfortunately, exposure to toxins, chemicals, heavy metals, poor nutrition, and other environmental factors disrupts their systems.

Toxins and chemicals can also be passed down ancestrally. For example, a mother's exposure to harmful substances whilst pregnant, may pass onto her unborn child, causing neurological or behavioural challenges. Barbara O'Neill talks about this in her book *Sustain Me*. She explains that although our DNA may plant the seed, our lifestyle still determines how it grows. Environmental exposure, including chemicals, heavy metals, vaccinations, EMFs, mould, food allergens, or emotional stress, can trigger inflammatory responses, autoimmune diseases, or neurodiverse symptoms.

Highly sensitive humans absorb these disturbances, and when we combine this with genetic traits, neurological and behavioural issues can manifest. Medications, processed foods, and environmental toxins further complicate matters. Some medications and vaccines contain heavy metals, toxins, and other substances that sensitive individuals may react to severely. Behavioural issues, allergies, and physical symptoms often reflect the body's attempt to communicate imbalance. Healing energy can support the body, but reducing exposure to harmful substances is essential for lasting results.

I have had sessions with numerous clients whose neurodiverse symptoms improved after clearing toxins and negative energies. One toddler, who regressed after a series of vaccines, regained communication and improved behavioural responses after healing sessions. Another child with autistic traits, ADHD, and sleep issues showed significant improvement following energy healing to remove chemicals and heavy metals. Even adults with autoimmune conditions, like Crohn's disease, can benefit from understanding the energetic impact of medications and chemicals.

So many health, behavioural, and sensitivity issues stem from the substances we consume or are exposed to. Awareness of ingredients, environmental factors, and energetic influences is crucial for self-healing and balance.

Below, I have included healing activations specifically designed to support neurodiverse conditions. While these activations alone may not fully resolve all imbalances, they are powerful tools to clear burdens, realign energy, and support individuals in feeling fully seen, heard, and safe.

Energy Clearing Activation for Autism

Take a deep breath and feel your body relax, put your hands on your heart and repeat this out loud:

You are made of divine intelligence.
You are not broken or a problem to fix.
You are filled with pure and clear multidimensional light.
God, release any spirits of distortion, confusion, misdiagnosis, or fear.

Spirit clear any unnecessary heavy metals, toxins, and chemicals, impacting the system.
I release inherited programming from the matrix that says you are wrong.
We take you to the light and bring you into the love of God.
I release and clear all energetic systems that were overwhelmed by density and restore ease to the nervous system.
I ask the spirit of my body to integrate light at a loving pace.
Spirit of the emotions, we ask you to bring peace and inner safety now.
Spirit of communication, we ask you to be restored.
Spirit of play, we ask you to be activated.
Spirit of joy, we ask you to be reawakened in this field.
I speak to the family line.
Any contracts of misunderstanding, suppression, or fear,
I release you now in the name of divine love.
And I declare this soul is sovereign.
This soul is seen.
This soul is whole.
And so it is.

ADHD Healing Activation

Take a deep breath, and with your hands on your heart, say the following out loud:

Spirit of divine intelligence,
Spirit of my mind,
Spirit of my energy body,
I now call you into full alignment with love.
To every part of me that feels too much, too fast, too scattered.
You are powerful.
You are connected energetically for greatness.
You are here to break the rules of limitation.

I call back my energy from every diagnosis that made me feel inadequate and unworthy and ask spirit to clear all chemicals, toxins, and heavy metals, disturbing my system.
I release all spirits of confusion, self-judgment, and shame.
I now take you to the light and bring you into the love of God.
Spirit of my nervous system, I love you. I speak peace to you and bring you balance.
I give you permission to operate in harmony with divine timing.
Mind you are not broken.
You are brilliant.
You are multidimensional and sovereign.
You are safe to focus.
Safe to rest.
Safe to thrive.
I release the need to prove anything to anyone.
I release the need to force things in order to be worthy.
I choose grace, presence, and joyful expression.
Spirit of joy, return to my body.
Spirit of divine order, activate in my energy field.
Spirit of creativity, guide me now.
And so it is.

ODD and Behavioural Healing Activation

This activation will call in clarity, release confusion, and restore sovereignty where your spirit felt forced to fight.

Put your hand on your heart, then breath in and out gently and speak the following out loud:

Spirit of truth and spirit of protection, I honour the part of me that said, 'No more.'
I now speak to the spirit of resistance. You are safe.
You no longer need to defend what is already divine.
I release the spirit of punishment and defiance.
I release any imprint of authority that was abusive or unloving.

I now take you to the light and bring you into the love of God. Every time the soul had to scream to be heard or the body felt trapped in a lie and every moment of chaos mistaken for identity.
I now offer healing, truth, and restoration.
Spirit of my nervous system, I love you.
You no longer need protection to feel powerful.
I restore peace within you and ease to your reactions.
Spirit of love, move through this field.
Spirit of joy, return to this body.
Spirit of safety, wrap around this mind, body, emotions and spirit.
I now speak to the root of this behaviour and say that you are free to be seen without needing to fight.
You are free to be powerful without needing to push.
You are free to soften without losing your power.
Spirit please clear all heavy metals, toxins, and chemicals that have been interfering with my system.
This soul is safe and loved.
This soul is sovereign and whole.
And so it is.

Chapter 15 – The Importance of Healing Sensitive Souls

The energetic health and vibration of our planet needs to rise if it is to remain healthy and thriving. I intuitively feel that this is why we are seeing more young souls born with remarkable sensitivity and empathy.

Mother Earth, along with the people and animals on her, cannot continue to exist as they are at present. The frequency of energy is so dense. The only way for improvement and change to occur is for these highly evolved, spiritual souls to incarnate here on Earth, helping to heal and raise the collective frequency. The challenge is that many of these high-frequency souls are highly sensitive to the current way of life, the harmful substances in what we consume, the heavy metals, chemicals, and toxins we are exposed to from the moment we are born. This, as I mentioned in Chapter 14, helps explain the rise in allergies, intolerances, and behavioural issues among young people.

More and more individuals are coming to me with challenges related to their sensitivity. Their sensitive bodies and energy systems require pure, clear energy, which our modern world struggles to provide.

I believe that many people born from the 1970s onwards chose to incarnate at this particular point in history to bring about change. They have chosen to come to Earth to channel their passion and drive into building the foundations for a healthier, more compassionate, harmonious, and healed society. Their purpose is to create a more peaceful, loving planet where humanity can continue to exist, heal, and thrive. These kinds of souls are often referred to as *Star Children*. I recognise myself as one of these children because many of the attributes resonate with me, which has helped me understand myself more deeply. I definitely see some attributes also in my own children.

When connecting with the higher realms, I was intuitively guided that there are three main types of souls who have been incarnating for some time to create positive, healing change, and three more who have arrived more recently with additional attributes, making a total of six.

To give a brief understanding: *Star Children* is a term used within spiritual and metaphysical communities to describe individuals with a special connection to the universe. They often possess unique abilities, heightened intuition, or a sense of purpose centred around helping humanity evolve. These souls are believed to originate from other star systems, dimensions, or spiritual realms, incarnating on Earth to guide, heal, and elevate human consciousness.

While these concepts are spiritual rather than scientifically proven, I, along with many other spiritual healers, mentors, and teachers, have intuitively received this guidance from higher realms. Many of my clients, including myself, resonate strongly with the attributes of *Star Children*. Understanding these traits can help explore a sense of purpose, personal characteristics, or spiritual experiences, as *Star Children* often display distinct energy, behaviour, and spiritual awareness.

Many clients reach out to me for themselves or their children, who fall under the *Star Child* categories. After healing sessions, they often feel lighter, and life seems easier to manage. This is because highly spiritual individuals require regular energetic clearing; without it, they can experience physical, emotional, and mental strain.

While interpretations may vary, the following are common attributes associated with *Star Children* to help you recognise and understand them better:

1.Heightened Intuition

Star Children often possess strong intuitive abilities, sensing things beyond the physical realm and understanding situations on a deeper, energetic level.

2.Empathy and Sensitivity

They are highly sensitive to the emotions and energies of others, as well as their environment. This can make them compassionate and nurturing but also prone to emotional overwhelm.

3.Feeling Like Outsiders

Many *Star Children* feel as though they do not 'fit in' with mainstream society, as if they are different or do not fully belong on Earth.

4.Wisdom Beyond Their Years

They may demonstrate a deep sense of insight or understanding from a young age, as if carrying ancient knowledge.

5.Strong Sense of Purpose

Star Children often feel they are here for a specific mission, such as healing others, protecting the planet, or helping to raise collective consciousness.

6.Creative and Visionary

They tend to be highly creative, with unique approaches to thinking, problem-solving, or self-expression, often through art, music, writing, or innovative ideas.

7.Challenging Authority

Particularly with *Indigo Children*, there can be a natural resistance to authority or rigid systems perceived as unjust or outdated.

8.Connection to Nature and the Cosmos

Some feel a profound bond with the natural world, animals, or the stars, and may be fascinated by cosmic or spiritual concepts.

9.Strong Ethical Principles

Star Children usually possess a heightened sense of justice and fairness, feeling compelled to stand up for truth and protect others.

10.Unusual Experiences

They may report spiritual encounters, vivid dreams, or experiences of communicating with higher beings or energies.

While these traits are commonly associated with *Star Children*, they can also reflect broader spiritual growth and personal development. Recognising these qualities can help understand your own sensitivity or that of someone you know.

I mentioned *Indigo Children* above, so I will now explore in more detail the specific types of children who fall under the umbrella of *Star Children*.

Indigo Children

The term *Indigo children* was popularised in the 1970s and 1980s by Nancy Ann Tappe, a parapsychologist who claimed she could perceive auras. She observed that many children born during this time had an indigo-coloured aura, which she associated with traits like intuition, independence, and a strong sense of purpose.

The concept gained wider attention with the 1999 book *The Indigo Children: The New Kids Have Arrived* by Lee Carroll and Jan Tober, which described these children as spiritually advanced beings here to help transform the world.

These children started to incarnate from around the 1920s, with numbers increasing significantly in the 1970s through to the 1990s.

They began to incarnate in the 1920s in order to initiate global shifts in consciousness. The first *Indigos* were seen as pioneers, quietly preparing the groundwork for future societal and spiritual transformations.

The number of *Indigo children* is thought to have increased during the 1960s - 1970s. This aligned with social movements advocating for freedom, civil rights, and global change. They were the spiritual warriors who broke down old ideals and created the hippy flower-power love scene and anti-war practices.

From the 1980s - 1990s, it was considered the peak period for *Indigo* incarnations, as many children born during this time exhibited traits like strong-willed independence, a desire to challenge unjust systems, and heightened intuition. They came to challenge and break outdated systems.

It's important to note that these timelines are based on spiritual and metaphysical interpretations, not scientific evidence. However, many people resonate with these ideas as a way to understand their personal traits, their sense of purpose, or feelings of being 'different' in the world.

Crystal Children

After 1992, it is believed that a wave of *Crystal Children* began to incarnate. The concept of *Crystal Children* started circulating in the 1990s and early 2000s, particularly through Doreen Virtue, who was a well-known figure in the spiritual community, although she no longer practices spirituality due to converting solely to Christianity.

Crystal Children are seen as having softer, more peaceful, nurturing, gentle, empathetic, and sensitive qualities. They often have a deep connection to nature and radiate a calm, harmonious energy. They incarnated to continue the work of transformation, with a focus on healing and harmony.

Their mission is to help build the foundation for a new society, one in which we may eventually all live in peace and goodwill. They came here to heal emotional wounds by bringing compassionate qualities of healing through love, fostering peace, empathy, and understanding.

Rainbow Children

The concept of *Rainbow Children* emerged in the late 1990s and early 2000s. It was frequently discussed and expanded upon again by Doreen Virtue in her teachings before she moved away from spirituality and converted to Christianity.

Rainbow Children began to incarnate on Earth in small numbers during the late 1990s and became more prominent from the early 2000s onwards. Their presence has increased significantly since 2010. They are joyful, highly energetic, and spiritually gifted souls, here to continue the work of healing and uplifting humanity, guiding us toward higher consciousness and ascension.

They often possess creative manifestation abilities and can bring their desires into reality very easily. *Rainbow Children* help us to reconnect with our higher selves and the spiritual realm, teaching us about unconditional love. By aligning with love as a society, we can create a happier world filled with peace, harmony, and less separation.

These children are here to embody unconditional love, joy, and harmony, and to heal, uplift, and balance the Earth's energy.

They are also thought to be born to spiritually aware parents (often *Crystal* adults) and are seen as highly intuitive, fearless, and naturally attuned to higher vibrations.

The challenge with *Rainbow Children* is that they require nurturing, and their carers need to understand their unique gifts in order to support them in a world that can feel heavy and dense. Carers must also be mindful of their health, avoiding toxins, heavy metals, and other harmful substances, because these sensitive children are highly attuned to energy imbalances, which can affect their wellbeing.

Violet Children

From 2012, *Violet Crystal Children* began to incarnate, inspired once again by the work of authors such as Nancy Ann Tappe and Doreen Virtue. These children share many of the attributes and heightened sensitivity of *Crystal Children*, but they also have additional tasks. They are here to heal and repair Earth's energetic grids, which support the Planet's life force. This helps to balance energy, and accelerate the healing and spiritual development of humanity.

Violet Crystal Children are seen as healers and spiritual guides, able to transmute negative energy, uplift consciousness, and inspire positive change. Their purpose is to bring peace, spiritual clarity, and emotional healing to the world.

Diamond Children

In 2015, *Diamond Children* began to incarnate on Earth, inspired once again by the work of Nancy Ann Tappe and later expanded upon by Doreen Virtue and other spiritual teachers. These children are considered new-world teachers, often referred to as Avatars. They possess very high levels of physical energy and stamina and are frequently labelled as having ADHD, as I discussed in the previous chapter. This can be challenging, as many of them are simply trying to express themselves in the only way they know how.

Diamond Children may also struggle to express or process dense emotions, such as anger or fear, because these feelings are unfamiliar to them. As a result, they are sometimes labelled as autistic. Verbal communication can be delayed, but they often communicate telepathically or through energy, which again can be misinterpreted as a form of autism. This is simply their natural way of connecting and understanding the world. Their telepathic gifts allow them to fully sense what others are feeling or thinking without words.

These children share a strong bond with nature, the cosmos, and universal consciousness, often demonstrating a wisdom and maturity far beyond their years.

The Golden Age Children

Following on from the other *Star Children* introduced by Nancy Ann Tappe and Doreen Virtue, the *Golden Age Children* began to incarnate in significant numbers in the late 2010s and early 2020s, although some spiritual sources suggest that a few may have arrived earlier to prepare the way. They are often associated with the Golden Age or the Age of Aquarius, a period believed to bring higher consciousness, unity, and enlightenment to humanity.

These children have come to show us how to raise our vibrations and expand our consciousness. They naturally radiate high-frequency energy, uplifting those around them and promoting oneness, helping humanity to move beyond division and towards collective healing. Many are natural healers, working with energy, empathy, or other forms of healing, and often act as spiritual teachers even from a young age.

Golden Age Children carry little or no karma and are highly intuitive and gifted. One of their challenges, however, is that they often become bored in traditional school environments. They possess a unique intelligence and need to be nurtured appropriately, otherwise they can struggle within outdated education systems. When supported in the right way, these children are incredibly intelligent and capable, yet their gifts can be misunderstood because basic education fails to engage them and they can be labelled as having traits that align with neurodiversity.

It is vital that parents and carers of *Star Children* or highly spiritual children understand why these children are here. This is why I felt it was so important to include this chapter in my book. Even if you are not a *Star Child* yourself, you are likely to know one who could benefit from your understanding, guidance, and support.

Changes Over the Next Decade Within Healing and Humanity

We will be moving fully into the fifth dimension by 2032. These children are here to teach us that it's the heart that guides us, and that unconditional love, oneness, and joy are all we truly need to be happy, connected, and healed.

It's rare for most of us to operate in a completely selfless, loving, and joyful way all the time. As babies, we naturally behave with innocence and unconditional love. But as we grow into adults, experiences and societal conditioning shape our thinking, and the feeling of oneness fades. I often find it strange how so many people walk past strangers without a smile or a hello, forgetting that we all came from Source and are connected.

We need to nurture these special souls and also heal ourselves, so we can relate to and accept these changes more easily. The

Golden Children are here as ambassadors of love, joy, peace, and oneness. These souls are our teachers, perhaps the most profound teachers we have had, guiding us to heal ourselves and our planet.

As time goes on, I believe more people will experience spiritual awakenings, leading to a greater collective understanding of unity, love, and higher-dimensional realities. This will make the process of moving into higher consciousness smoother. We'll also see psychic and intuitive abilities increasing, and it will become more common and normal to recognise and use these gifts as humanity reconnects with its true nature.

By 2032, more people will be aware of spiritually advanced souls, like the *Golden Age, Diamond,* and *Rainbow Children*, all of whom will play key roles in guiding the planet toward a more harmonious existence.

As humanity begins to embrace new ways of thinking and healing, the old systems will naturally collapse. Traditional societal structures built on fear, control, and separation will continue to fall apart. I truly hope a new heart-centred approach to leadership, education, and healing will emerge to replace our outdated systems. We are moving from a 3D reality, based on separation and ego, to a 5D consciousness of unity, love, and expanded awareness. There is evidence that the Earth is experiencing shifts in energy, and there will continue to be more solar activity, and planetary alignments contributing to this transformation, helping the planet align with these higher frequencies.

I also believe we'll see advancements in both holistic and energy-based healing methods becoming more integrated into mainstream medicine. Some NHS clinics in the UK already offer Reiki as part of their complimentary therapy services, and in the future, I hope that we may see sound healing, quantum healing, and other modalities, complementing traditional medical practices. This would be a very positive step toward holistic well-being.

The spiritual teacher Diana Cooper specifically points to 2032 in her book, *Transition to the Golden Age in 2032*, as a key milestone in the Planet's transition into the Golden Age. While interpretations vary, the common theme is a profound transformation toward greater love, wisdom, and consciousness.

I am very excited to see what happens over the next decade in healing and humanity. Although it may feel as if systems are crumbling, sometimes they must fall apart in order to make space for better, more heart-centred structures. The sooner older generations change their perceptions and rigid ways of thinking, the more these special souls will feel accepted.

As these children grow, they will transform the world in a profoundly positive way, but they need guidance and support. *Indigo* and *Crystal children*, now adults, also need encouragement to find their purpose. That's why I am so passionate about reaching younger audiences on social media. Many 'lost souls' in society are actually *Star Children* who feel misunderstood. Raising awareness of these wonderful humans and their gifts will help create a happier, more loving planet.

As these new generations continue to incarnate and grow, their high frequency of oneness and wholeness will reduce the lower vibrations and challenges we often bring into the world. What a truly beautiful, healthy, healed, and loving world it will be!

Chapter 16 – Psychic Attack on the Body

We've all experienced a psychic attack at some point in our lives, whether we were aware of it or not. This can be as simple as someone projecting jealousy, anger, or a bad mood onto you, sometimes intentionally, sometimes without even realising it. You might not even be aware that their energy has affected you, leaving your system open to negative influences.

While we are all familiar with physical harm or harsh words and their emotional effects, many people do not recognise the impact of energetic harm. Negative thoughts and intentions from others can create imbalance on every level, mental, emotional, spiritual, and even physical.

A psychic attack occurs when negative energy, thoughts, or intentions from another person, or occasionally an external entity, interfere with your energy field. These attacks can be subtle or intense, but their effects can be profound.

Psychic Attack Symptoms

You may notice some of the following signs:

1. Sudden Fatigue or Low Energy – Feeling drained without a clear physical reason.
2. Intrusive Negative Thoughts – Anxiety, fear, or self-doubt that feels unnatural.
3. Unexplained Physical Symptoms – Headaches, nausea, or body aches without a medical cause.

4. Disturbed Sleep – Nightmares, sleep paralysis, or waking up exhausted.
5. Unusual Misfortunes or Bad Luck – A streak of negativity that feels unnatural.

Examples of Psychic Attack

- A colleague who was competing for the same job and did not get it may feel resentful, angry, or jealous. Their energy can reflect this negativity.
- An ex-partner who harbours bitterness or resentment, even years after a breakup, may unconsciously project this energy onto you. Everyone has some darkness within them, and when negative feelings are not acknowledged or released, they can affect others.
- Envy surrounding your career, relationships, or social status can create subtle energetic attacks.
- Social media interactions can trigger psychic attacks. A simple post may provoke jealousy or resentment in someone, which can transmit negative energy to you.
- An individual living in fear, depression, or self-doubt may unintentionally project these low vibrations onto others.

The Effects of Psychic Attack

Although science does not currently provide evidence for psychic attacks, many spiritual practitioners, metaphysical authors, and esoteric texts document experiences of energy transfer. Thought and intention carry energy, which can influence another person's aura or energy field.

Every person has an energy field surrounding them, reflecting their physical, emotional, and spiritual state. When a psychic attack occurs, it can disrupt this field, causing fatigue, emotional instability, or even physical symptoms.

If someone consciously sends negative energy with the intention of causing harm, the energy they project is eventually returned to them, often amplified, through the universal law of karma.

Avoiding Repercussions

It is essential not to retaliate with negative energy.

Responding with anger, fear, or resentment only intensifies the situation. Instead:

- Trust that the universe will handle the situation.
- Send love and compassion to the individual. Visualise hugging them or surrounding them with healing light.
- Maintain emotional stability and inner strength, which makes it less likely for negative energy to affect you.

The high vibrations of love, kindness, and forgiveness can neutralise low-energy attacks, transforming negativity into positive energy. Staying grounded, energetically healthy, and emotionally resilient is your most powerful protection.

Psychic Attack Protection Technique

You can learn to protect yourself from psychic attacks or negative energy.

Try the following exercise:

1. Morning Energy Cleansing – Each morning, ask your angels, guides, ancestors, or spirit to cleanse and clear your energy field. Request that any energy cords linking

you to people or situations be cut. This helps release negative attachments and energetic ties.

2. Visualise Protection – Once your energy field has been cleared, imagine a protective black cloak being placed around you, complete with a hood for extra security. Alternatively, you can visualise an invisible barrier surrounding your body.
3. Ask for Protection – Ask your angels, guides, ancestors, or spirit to keep you safe from any external harm. If you feel out of balance, request that all psychic attack be removed. If you believe you know who is projecting lower-frequency energy towards you, send them love rather than respond with anger or upset. Visualise hugging them or sending loving energy. The frequency of love neutralises negative energy.

It is also essential to maintain a high vibration by thinking and speaking positively, practising gratitude, and surrounding yourself with uplifting energy. These habits strengthen your energy field and make it far less likely for negativity to affect you.

Psychic Attack Healing Activation

If you feel that you've experienced a psychic attack and are feeling panicky or out of sorts, you can try the following healing activation.

Stand with both hands on your heart and say out loud:

Spirit of protection, flow through me now.
Fire Spirits burn through every projection, attachment, and curse not of God.
No fear, attack or distortion can enter, hide or stay.

I now ask every spirit of fear, confusion, manipulation, or control,
to move over to the light and into the love of God.
I am surrounded by divine protection.
My energy is mine.
My field is strong.
I say yes to my pure light and safety.

Chapter 17 – Earthbound Spiritual Attachments

Spiritual attachments are non-physical energies, entities, or thought forms that attach themselves to a person's energy field or aura. These attachments can influence our emotions, thoughts, and overall energy, sometimes positively, but more often than not, negatively. They can have a profound impact on our healing journey.

Authors such as Barbara Brennan, Robert Bruce, and Dion Fortune have all written about spiritual attachments. In Dion Fortune's 1930 book *Psychic Self-Defence*, she discussed how negative energies and psychic influences could attach to a person. Similar concepts appear across various religious and mystical traditions, spanning centuries.

To clarify, past experiences, traumas, or unresolved emotions can leave energetic imprints and residues. Over time, these imprints may attach themselves to a person, subtly affecting behaviour or emotional state unless the energy is healed.

Beyond internal factors, external entities, whether spirits, guides, or so called 'energy vampires,' can attach to a person. These attachments often result from intentional or unintentional interactions, such as during intense emotional or spiritual exchanges.

The effects of spiritual attachments vary. Some individuals report feeling drained, experiencing unexplained emotional turmoil, or noticing patterns in their behaviour that seem influenced by an external presence. I will discuss my observations with clients in more detail later in this chapter.

Spirit attachments can occur within the aura, at the nexus gateway portal, in the solar plexus within the chakra system, or even in the physical body. The spirit or entity latches onto some part of the client's energy field.

Most earthbound spirits are usually innocent, seeking comfort because they haven't fully transitioned to the spirit world. They may linger between dimensions, feeling unworthy of moving to a higher plane, and often attach themselves to a living human's energy field unless helped over to the light.

However, dark-force entities, lower vibrational spirits, also exist. These entities attach themselves to living people with the intention of creating fear, misery, and despair, draining the person's life-force energy. Fortunately, these dark-force entities are usually easy to guide to the light during a healing session and can be cleared relatively quickly.

When I do healing sessions with a client and detect an attachment, I ask it to cross over to the light, assisting it to move peacefully and safely. Sometimes this takes only a single attempt, though on occasion, the attachment may resist, requiring additional sessions. I have also seen clients improve, then regress weeks or months later. This has created the need for another clearing, as lingering or new attachments may arrive if the client is still experiencing trauma, stress, or anxiety. Spiritual attachments often occur when the aura is weakened due to physical or emotional trauma.

I once did sessions with two particularly troubled clients, both self-harming and experiencing suicidal thoughts. After addressing their specific issues and clearing the attachments affecting their mind and emotions, we observed remarkable improvements. Sometimes, individuals with severe struggles are not fully in control of their actions, and the attachments are influencing their behaviour.

In one case, after releasing an attachment from a young woman, she experienced a noticeable transformation. Her family noticed a positive shift in her personality. She became happier, more optimistic, and after a year of inactivity, she began seeking employment. Her mother even said she felt she had her daughter back. Once the attachment was fully released, her thought processes shifted, and she began feeling like herself again.

Many clients notice unusual symptoms or feel extremely fatigued. It's important to understand that this is different from psychic attacks. While it's completely normal to experience occasional bouts of anger, sadness, or illness, persistent or unusual feelings may point to a spiritual attachment. This isn't a medical diagnosis, so it's always essential to rule out any underlying health issues. Some clients have described cravings they wouldn't normally have, changes in eating habits, a sense of disconnection from their body, or difficulty focusing. In more extreme cases, people may experience thoughts of self-harm or even harming others, which could potentially be linked to an attachment.

Nine times out of ten, I find an attachment when checking a client's energy field. If none is present, this allows me to rule out attachments and intuitively investigate other causes.

When spiritually healing a client, I always ask my divine healing team to clear any earthbound spiritual attachments and dark entities, visualising these entities being safely and peacefully guided to the light. I have included a clearing exercise later in this chapter that you can practise regularly to prevent attachments. By performing this exercise, you are not only protecting yourself but also helping these spirits transition safely over to the light. Often, once they move on, they continue to assist and support you from the spiritual realms. A win-win for both parties.

Spiritual Attachment Clearing Activation

You can say this Activation out loud or in your head:

Spirit, take me higher above my suffering and clear me of all spiritual attachments.
Take me so high that nothing negative can hold onto me.
Thank you Angels.
You have no power here, spiritual attachments, move over to the light.
Superconscious, correct any imbalances that were created in my life and recode and align me to more beneficial energies.
Thank you God.
It is done.

Note: sometimes spirit attachments can really resist when you do an activation to clear them. If this happens, then ask spirit, to move the spirit of resistance over to the light and into the love of God, and then repeat the activation until you feel a shift.

Chapter 18 – Clearing and Cleansing the Aura and Energy Field

Just as it is incredibly important to protect and care for your physical body, it is equally crucial to nurture and safeguard your energetic body.

If the energetic body is not cared for regularly, it can become congested, which may profoundly affect your physical, emotional, and mental well-being.

Your aura is the energetic force that surrounds your entire body. It acts like a magnet, drawing in and repelling the emotions, psychic debris, and energy that float around you. In fact, you don't just have one aura; you have many. Your spirit, mind, emotions, and body all radiate their own auric layers.

The health and vitality of your aura shapes the filter through which you experience the world. When your auric field is healthy, balanced, and strong, you feel energised, positive, and aligned with your soul. But when you are under stress, unwell, or your immune system is low, your auric field can weaken. This can leave you feeling drained, emotional, negative, and off balance.

Our auras are constantly interacting. They overlap and connect with the energetic fields of others around us. Energetic cords also attach us to people we are connected to, which means we can feel the frequencies of those nearby. If we spend time with people who are negative, angry, or sad, our own energy can become destabilised. The same happens within the home.

Unresolved arguments or heavy emotions can linger in the atmosphere, creating imbalance. Even neighbouring energies can seep through the walls if we share space with stressed or angry neighbours.

Over time, these influences may contribute to issues such as fatigue, anxiety, or depression. I see this often in children, as I mentioned in a previous chapter. Many children today are born highly sensitive, and because they are immersed daily in the energies of classmates, teachers, and family members, their fields can easily become overwhelmed.

Reasons Your Aura May Need Cleansing

- Being around large numbers of people (for example, on a crowded train, in a busy city, or in an office environment).
- Feeling depleted after a traumatic or exhausting event.
- Being highly stressed or chronically tired.
- Spending time around negative, fearful, or stressed individuals.

Emotional Sponges

We often absorb energy without even realising it, which causes us to become emotional sponges.

Imagine yourself on a packed commuter train. Your aura is overlapping with dozens of strangers, some of whom may be having a difficult day. Their energy projects onto you and suddenly you feel anxious, agitated, or drained, even though you started the morning in a perfectly good mood.

This is more common than people think. During the Covid-19 outbreak, many clients experienced overwhelming waves of fear that were not truly their own. One client told me she felt fine when leaving for the supermarket, but while shopping she suffered a panic attack and had to leave. She remained anxious and dizzy for hours afterwards. When she contacted me, I could sense instantly that what she was experiencing was not her own energy, but rather the collective fear of those around her. Through prayer, visualisation, and energy healing, we cleared her field, and within a few hours she felt back to herself again.

This is why it's so vital to remain aware of the role your energetic field plays in your life, and to care for it with regular cleansing.

Cleansing Aura Exercise

Cleansing your aura is simple and can be done daily to help you feel vibrant, strong, and clear. You might also wish to include your family, as even children benefit from learning these gentle practices.

- **Ask** your guides, angels, or spirit team to remove any energetic debris that may be affecting you. It really can be as simple as asking.
- **Take** a cleansing bath and invite the water spirits to clear your aura. Add sea salt, eucalyptus, or lavender for at least ten minutes to stimulate energy flow. Himalayan salt is also excellent for releasing unwanted energy. Alternatively, take a shower and imagine golden healing light flowing through the water, washing away negativity.
- **Connect** with nature. Walk barefoot on grass or sand, place your feet in the sea, or hug a tree. All of these help to neutralise energy.
- **Sit** in sunlight and ask the fire spirits to burn away any negative residue.
- **Stand** in the wind and ask the wind spirits to carry away any stagnant energy.

Fan Technique

This is a more physical method of clearing your aura:

1. **Stand** with your feet grounded.
2. **Begin fanning** the energy around your body, staring at your feet and moving upwards. Ensure that you are pushing the unwanted energy away from all sides of your body in order to remove it.
3. **Visualise** light waves clearing your aura if it feels difficult to reach behind you.
4. **Continue fanning** until you reach above your head, then **push** the energy outwards and **shake** it down into the earth.

Box Technique

After cleansing your aura, it's important to protect it from external negativity. Surrounding yourself with uplifting people will naturally help, but you can also use this visualisation:

1. **Ask** your spiritual team to clear any remaining energy that is not your own.
2. **Imagine** stepping into a strong metal box.
3. **Envision** the box lined with platinum, and covered with mirrors. The reflective surfaces will bounce any unwanted energy away from you.
4. **Place** a lid on the box and see yourself fully enclosed and protected.

Repeat this daily to keep your vibration high and your aura strong.

Aura Cleansing Light Activation

You can use this short activation prayer to create a quick cleansing.

Say in your mind or out loud:

Spirit of divine purity, I now cleanse my aura in your light.
Every layer of my field, physical, emotional, mental, and spiritual is now cleared.
I release all cords, projections, and attachments that do not serve my highest truth.
I send back what is not mine and call home every fragment of my energy.
Recalibrate my aura to clarity, joy, strength, and sovereignty.
Spirit of my emotions, lift my frequency to peace.
Spirit of my body, seal my field with vibrant vitality.
I am now shielded with protection.
I say yes to feeling fully restored.

Chapter 19 – Crystals as Frequency Medicine

I want to touch briefly on crystals. These beautiful gifts from Earth, have been here long before us, holding powerful medicine. Each crystal carries its own unique vibration, offering balance, healing, and a reminder of the light within each of us.

We live in a world that can often feel noisy, busy, and overwhelming to our energy. Crystals act like tuning forks, bringing us back into balance. They can sharpen our clarity, calm emotional overwhelm, reveal deeper truths, and strengthen the boundaries that keep us steady and protected.

They don't heal us directly. Instead, they hold a frequency that allows the body to remember its divine blueprint. When your energy feels chaotic and your emotions feel overwhelming, they restore and stabilise. When the mind spirals into negativity and energies linger around us, they ground and protect us.

They are incredibly powerful allies for maintaining optimum health and balance in the human body.

In my own healing practice, I often connect with crystals, and feel intuitively guided toward the ones a client needs for their unique journey. There are thousands of stones, each with its own gifts.

Below, I've shared just a few of the most common crystals and their benefits:

Common Crystals and Their Benefits

Rose Quartz

- The crystal of unconditional love
- It softens the heart
- Fantastic crystal for love and bringing love of self, others and any situations needing love
- Helps to feel calm, harmonious and peaceful and creates emotional healing
- Releases stress
- Promotes circulation
- Skin health
- Great for the parent-child relationships and family bonding
- Dispels anger, jealousy and resentment
- Good for resolving any issues of the heart

Citrine

- A stone of abundance and vitality
- Enhances physical stamina and energy
- Supports the endocrine system and encourages proper metabolism
- Good for chronic fatigue syndrome
- Balances the thyroid
- Good for happiness, optimism and abundance, wealth and prosperity
- Helps achieve goals
- Absorbs negative energy
- Promotes creativity and imagination
- Purges toxins
- Strengthens confidence
- Helps release fears around scarcity
- Uplifts the mood

Amethyst

- A stone of peace and spiritual protection
- Brings calmness and clarity
- Helps calm and relax the nervous system
- Removes toxins from the blood
- Reduces scattered thoughts and helps focus
- Reduces headaches
- Balances hormones
- Helps think more creatively
- Boosts intuition
- Raises your vibration to feel more love, compassion and joy
- Supports restful sleep

Clear Quartz

- The master healer
- Improves memory
- Increases intuition
- Amplifies energy and accelerates intention and healing processes
- Improves awareness
- Aids in creativity
- Promotes clarity
- Can be programmed for almost any purpose

Obsidian

- Powerful cleanser
- Shields against negativity
- Relieves pain of arthritis and cramps
- Dissolves emotional blocks
- Grounding stone
- Helps us channel answers from spirit and our higher selves
- Shields from psychic attack

- Good for growth and power
- Deep soul healing stone

Black Tourmaline

- It anchors when the nervous system is scanning for danger
- Acts like a vibrational shield
- Deflects psychic attack
- Deflects EMF electromagnetic frequencies
- Clears jealousy and projection
- Clears energetic residue from other people
- Grounds your energy field
- Give you spiritual boundary support
- Repels lower frequencies

Shungite

- Neutralises toxins and EMFs
- Is a detoxifier both physically and energetically
- Balances the bodies bio field
- Restores cellular harmony
- Strengthens your light grid
- Reviews what's off, distorted, or hiding in the shadows
- It connects you to the deep earth
- Helps with trauma healing, grounding you after a spiritual journey, and reconnects you into your physical body

There are so many crystals to choose from, each with their own benefits. You don't need a large collection to feel the power of crystals. Often, one or two stones that you feel drawn to are more than enough. When selecting one, you'll often feel drawn to a particular colour, shape, or stone, and that's usually your higher self guiding you to the crystal you need most in that moment. Trust your intuition and the right crystal will always find its way to you.

There are countless ways to work with crystals. You might place them on your chakra points during meditation, keep one in your pocket, wear them as bracelets, tuck them under your pillow at night, or, like I sometimes do, slip one into your bra! However you choose to carry them, you'll soon notice how their presence begins to shift your energy.

One of the most important practices with crystals is cleansing them. Crystals absorb, echo, and amplify energy, so when you first receive one, it has likely been handled by others and is carrying residual vibrations that aren't yet aligned with you. Without cleansing, crystals can hold on to stress, fear, or stagnant patterns from their previous environment, which can make your own energy feel heavy or unsettled.

Crystals work best when their frequency is clear and they are vibrating as pure channels. Below are some simple cleansing methods you can try. See which ones feel right for you:

- **Smoke cleanse** – Wave palo santo, white sage, or frankincense smoke over your crystal, allowing the smoke to absorb and carry away unwanted energy.
- **Selenite charging** – Place your crystal in a selenite bowl or rest it against a selenite wand. Selenite is self-cleansing and naturally purifies other stones without needing to be cleared itself.
- **Sound bath** – Use a singing bowl, tuning fork, or chime. The sound vibrations break up stagnant energy and realign the crystal's natural structure.
- **Earth burial** – For deep cleansing, bury your crystal in the earth for 24 hours. This is especially powerful if the stone has been used for protection or trauma support, as the earth resets and restores its vibration.

Crystal Cleanse Activation

Say this activation whilst holding the chosen crystal that needs cleansing.

Spirit of this crystal, I thank you for your service.
Cleanse, clear, recalibrate.
You are now attuned to the frequency of love, protection, and purpose again.
And so it is.

Crystal Healing Activation

You can say this activation whilst holding your chosen crystal in your hands or placing it on a part of your body.

Spirit of this crystal,
I ask that you now radiate your divine intelligence into my being.
I give you permission to scan my body, mind, spirit and emotions.
To locate any energy that is out of harmony with my divine blueprint.
Dissolve interference and heaviness and replace it with lightness.
I am ready, I am open, I am aligned with your medicine.
I now receive your healing fully and completely within every cell of my body.
And so it is.

Remember, crystals are not just tools, they are allies. Treat them with care, gratitude, and respect, and they will respond by amplifying your own healing and clarity.

Chapter 20 – The Power of Symbols and Codes in Healing

Symbols and codes are powerful tools for communicating with the spiritual realms because they speak a language beyond the thinking mind. I've used them many times on myself and with clients, witnessing how they can reach directly into the subconscious and energy body, allowing old patterns and stored memories to shift and heal. They carry vibration and intention, especially when healing intentions are infused into them by the creator. I believe symbols and codes can spark real transformation, healing, and spiritual growth.

Often, I receive divine inspiration to create symbols and codes using numbers and colours, which I then use as healing tools for my clients. I've shared a few symbols and codes that I've created and infused with healing energy that you will find below. You can use these whenever you feel the need for extra support in any area of your life.

Images of Symbols

Instructions:

When focusing on a specific symbol, immerse yourself in its intricate patterns for about ten seconds, or for as long as you feel inclined, in order to sense its energy. While looking at the symbol, gently place your hand on your crown chakra (the centre at the top of your head), then tap your head three times.

As you tap, ask Spirit to download the healing energy into your four-body system (the mind, body, spirit and emotions).

You may feel a shift in frequency as you do this exercise. If you don't, that's perfectly fine, your body still receives what it needs. You can also ask Spirit to release any lower-frequency energy, as sometimes a lower vibration can temporarily block the full experience. This gentle clearing of lower frequencies allows you to receive the complete healing benefits.

Say out loud:

Spirit, please release any fear or lack of trust spirits and send them over to the light and into the love of God.

Then repeat the exercise.

Joy

Calm

Peace

Happiness

Good Luck

Self-Love

Healing Codes

You can download these codes into your system:

ABUNDANCE *- Download 724, and the colours blue, white, and magenta into your four-body system.*

TRUST *- Download 689, and the colours aqua blue, orange, purple, and white into your four-body system.*

SUCCESS *- Download 374, and the colours red, honey yellow, and silver grey into your four-body system.*

LOVE *- Download 871, and the colours gold, orange and turquoise, into your four-body system.*

HAPPINESS *- Download 94, and the colours amber, white, silver, purple, and orange into your four-body system.*

Chapter 21 – What Are Chakras and Why We Should Cleanse and Clear Them for Optimal Healing

Chakras are not widely discussed in Western society because there's no scientific evidence proving their existence as physical structures. However, they hold great meaning in spiritual and psychological contexts because they provide a framework for understanding and balancing the flow of energy in the body, mind, and spirit.

Without realising it, chakras play a huge role in our health, promoting harmony, emotional wellbeing, and personal growth. Unless you're spiritually minded, have studied other religions such as Hinduism or Tantric Buddhism, or practise yoga or pilates, you may not have heard of them before.

I first studied chakras several years ago after learning a little bit about them from a spiritual teacher. I then felt drawn to want to learn more about them, in order to understand how they affect my own energy.

Chakras are circular vortexes of energy located at different points along your spinal column. Each chakra connects to various organs and glands within the body and influences life energy. The chakras we work with most represent different areas of the body and affect not only physical health but also emotions, mindset, and spiritual wellbeing during our healing journey.

When I began learning about my chakras, my energy and overall wellbeing shifted positively in ways I had not expected.

While seven primary chakras are the most well-known, there are actually 114 chakras in total, forming a complex network of energy points throughout the body. The 114 chakras provide a more detailed energy map, allowing practitioners to achieve deeper levels of spiritual awakening, refine energy balance, enhance intuition, access altered states of consciousness, and clear blockages in less-known chakras to improve overall wellbeing.

Because this isn't a book dedicated solely to chakras, and given their vast number, I will focus on the most well-known chakras in simple terms to give you insight into how they can support your healing journey.

The Seven Major Chakras

These are the foundational energy centres, from the Root Chakra to the Crown Chakra, and are the chakras most people are familiar with.

- **Root Chakra (Muladhara) – Red**

Located at the base of the spine, associated with grounding, stability, and survival instincts.

- **Sacral Chakra (Svadhisthana) – Orange**

Found just below the navel, linked to creativity, emotions, and sexuality.

- **Solar Plexus Chakra (Manipura) – Yellow**

Situated in the upper abdomen, affecting confidence, personal power, and self-esteem.

- **Heart Chakra (Anahata) – Green**

Centre of the chest, associated with love, compassion, and emotional balance.

- **Throat Chakra (Vishuddha) – Blue**

Located at the throat, connected to communication and self-expression.

- **Third Eye Chakra (Ajna) – Indigo**

Positioned between the eyebrows, linked to intuition, insight, and higher consciousness.

- **Crown Chakra (Sahasrara) – Violet**

At the top of the head, representing spiritual connection and enlightenment.

The Root

The Root Chakra (red) is positioned at the base of the spinal column. It governs the lower body, including the bladder, kidneys, lower spine, and back, and psychologically oversees confidence and survival instincts.

When functioning well, you feel grounded, secure, and at ease with the world. When blocked or out of balance, you may experience constipation, bladder problems, kidney stones, leg weakness, back pain, and fatigue. Emotional signs include insecurity, restlessness, anger, aggressive behaviour, sexual dysfunction, impatience, greed, obsession with material matters, and eating disorders.

The Sacral

The Sacral Chakra (orange) is located in the lower abdomen, just below the navel. When balanced, it allows you to express creativity healthily, feel energetic, passionate, playful, warm, and generally happy.

When blocked, you may feel out of control, unemotional, uncertain, insecure, detached, or rigid in routines. Low self-esteem may result in unhealthy relationships and a general sense of imbalance.

The Solar Plexus

The Solar Plexus Chakra (yellow) is located two inches above the navel. When balanced, you trust yourself, follow your gut instincts, and confidently interact with others.

When blocked, you may struggle with indecision, low self-esteem, lack of boundaries, codependency, anxiety, depression, addiction, or an unhealthy need to control others. Physically you may have digestive discomfort, bloating, nausea, and memory issues.

The Heart

The Heart Chakra (green) is positioned in the centre of the chest. It bridges the lower and upper chakras, connecting the physical and spiritual self.

When balanced, it creates love, compassion, empathy, forgiveness, and the ability to form deep, meaningful relationships. When blocked it may manifest as emotional pain, heartbreak, and physical issues such as heart disease, lung and respiratory problems, breast cancer, upper back pain, or immune system dysfunction.

The Throat

The Throat Chakra (blue) is in the middle of the neck. A balanced throat chakra allows authentic self-expression, clear communication, creativity, and purpose.

Blockages here may lead to difficulty expressing needs, poor unresolved conflict, emotional dishonesty, or feeling unheard. Physical effects include sore throats, stiff neck, and hormonal fluctuations, often rooted in childhood experiences, where you were suppressed of expressing yourself.

The Third Eye

The Third Eye Chakra (indigo) is between the eyebrows and governs intuition, insight, and inner guidance.

When open, it enhances imagination, clairvoyance, self-awareness, and emotional balance. Blockages may result in paranoia, mood disorders, depression, anxiety, bitterness, distrust, or limited perspective.

The Crown

The Crown Chakra (violet or white) sits at the top of the head and connects us to universal consciousness.

A balanced crown chakra creates wisdom, connection, empathy, and contentment. Blockages may cause depression, disconnection, insomnia, materialism, mental fog, chronic fatigue, migraines, and neurological or endocrine issues.

Minor and Micro Chakras

Beyond the primary chakras, the human energy system includes:

- **21 Minor Chakras** – Located in joints, hands, feet, and specific organs, subtly influencing energy flow.
- **86 Micro Chakras** – Small energy points distributed throughout the body, fine-tuning physiological and energetic balance.

Chakras and Cosmic Consciousness

Certain chakras connect us to higher consciousness. Meditation, energy healing, and spiritual practice can strengthen these connections:

- **Crown Chakra (Sahasrara)** – Part of the primary seven chakras; links to universal energy and spiritual wisdom.
- **Soul Star Chakra** – Above the crown; enhances connection to cosmic consciousness and higher guidance.

Expanded systems also include Stellar Gateway Chakras, accessed through advanced energy work or spiritual intuition.

In my healing practice, I intuitively assess both primary and expanded chakras. When there is slow or stagnant energy in these areas, this often correlates with clients' challenges.

Many of us carry energetic stagnation or habits that sabotage vitality, leaving us drained, out of balance, or physically unwell. Understanding and maintaining chakra balance daily can restore vitality, wellbeing, and spiritual connection.

Daily Chakra Care

Simple daily practices support chakra health:

- **Meditation and visualisation** – Focus on each chakra's colour and energy flow.
- **Movement and yoga** – Release blocked energy and harmonise mind and body.
- **Affirmations and intention** – Align thoughts and statements with each chakra's purpose.
- **Energy healing tools** – Reiki, symbols, or codes to activate and clear blockages.

Even a few minutes daily can shift stagnant energy and improve physical, emotional, and spiritual wellbeing.

Visualising the Chakras

This diagram shows the seven chakras on the human body, illustrating the energy patterns moving upward from the root to the crown, highlighting the flow from grounding in the Earth to spiritual connection.

Human Chakra Mandala

Balancing Your Chakras

After deep emotional distress, it can be harder to bring your chakras back into balance. In some cases, extra help from a trained Reiki practitioner, spiritual healer, or energy and crystal healer can be beneficial, especially if you've experienced major physical, emotional, or spiritual trauma.

Luckily, you can also practice a quick chakra clearing, cleansing, and balancing activation yourself. Doing this regularly helps keep your energy flowing freely, so you feel energised, healthy, and aligned.

A rainbow has seven colours, just like the seven most well known chakras in your body.

You might have heard of the 'pot of gold at the end of the rainbow'. Think of your chakras as your own colorful rainbow: by keeping them balanced and vibrant, you create your own pot of gold within a life of success, fulfillment, and happiness.

The activation below is simple, fast, and powerful. Not only will it balance the seven main chakras, but it can also harmonise all 114 chakras throughout your energy field.

Chakra Balancing and Cleansing Activation

Follow these steps to cleanse and balance your chakras:

1. **Stand firmly** on the ground and place your left hand on your belly button to connect with your energy.
2. **Take a deep breath in.**
3. **Visualise** white-golden light entering from above your Crown, flowing down through your entire body.
4. **Repeat** this activation aloud or silently:

I am grounded, creative, powerful, loving, expressive, intuitive, and connected.
Spirit please expand my auric field and scan, heal, awaken and harmonise all 114 chakras.
Flood my energy field with pure light.
Realign all of my 114 chakras now across all timelines, ensuring that my whole energy field is healed and harmonised.
I am now aligned and vibrating with wholeness.
It is done.

5. Feel the energy moving. Imagine the divine light activating, harmonising, and aligning all 114 chakras, from your Root, through your Crown, deep into the Earth, and out into the cosmos.

During the activation, your body may respond in different ways. Common reactions include:

- **Yawning**
- **Sneezing**
- **Coughing**
- **Burping**
- **Crying**
- **Feeling a shudder of hot or cold energy**

These are normal signs that your energy is moving and clearing.

Keeping your chakras balanced and cleansed helps you maintain energy flow, clarity, and connection, your personal rainbow of power, creativity, love, and spiritual alignment.

Chapter 22 – The Key to Forgiveness and Acceptance in Order to Heal

I could have discussed this topic earlier in the book, but I wanted to conclude with this important chapter because I personally feel it is one of the most fundamental areas when it comes to healing. It is also one of the most important topics in our healing process.

It is an aspect I have definitely struggled with on my own healing journey, and I have found many of my clients have also struggled with the ability to fully and wholeheartedly forgive, accept, and let go of situations. This can involve other people and circumstances we face, but also the ability to forgive ourselves. I am still navigating this each time a test is thrown my way, but when I look back on my younger years, I feel I have come far in this aspect of my evolution. I am now far more aware of what triggers me and how to move through the energy without resistance.

I wanted to talk about this topic because we so often hear about the need to forgive, ourselves, others, or circumstances. Yet the real game-changer is not necessarily forgiveness, but rather acceptance. Accepting what has happened and recognising that, in order to move forward, we must let the situation or circumstance go, even if we cannot fully forgive.

Many of us replay negative scenarios over and over in our minds like a film, becoming increasingly agitated, resentful, and upset. This energy builds deep within us and can manifest as illness.

According to the late Louise Hay, holding onto resentment and an unwillingness to forgive can contribute to cancer, arthritis, liver problems, and heart conditions. I have also tuned into clients with abscesses and cysts, which manifested due to running painful thoughts over and over and fermenting feelings of hurt. Your emotions and thoughts are powerful, remember, you are a powerful manifestor.

There have been many occasions where I have been worked up and upset, whether with myself, another person, or a situation. Who did it affect? Not the people who I felt had wronged me, they probably had no idea. It only affected me.

We must break this cycle and free ourselves from the chains of situations and people that have affected us. These negative and destructive frequencies create dis-ease within the body.

A huge learning curve for me personally came when major, life-changing events occurred. They opened my eyes to who was truly present when the going got tough. It took me a long time to get over these experiences, but I realised that if I was to help others on their healing journey, I too needed to accept these experiences. Even if I could not completely forgive, acceptance was essential in order to move forward. How could I teach others to forgive or accept if I had not done so myself?

A few years ago, I was unfairly judged. Rather than respond with anger, resentment, or malice, I chose to walk away, send love, forgive, accept, and move on. Not because I condoned how I was treated, but because otherwise it would have consumed me negatively. I realised then how far I had come, because ten years earlier, I would have handled it very differently, holding onto the pain. A few days after the incident, I made the conscious decision to free myself from these negative energies and behaviours.

When I have healing sessions with clients to move stagnant, resentful energy in their energetic field, I cut the attachment cords between them and the person or situation that requires forgiveness. Huge shifts occur within their energy field because the ties and energies held in a circumstance are often connected by an energetic cord. Many clients instantly feel lighter once these cords are cut.

People come into our lives to teach us lessons, and once the lessons are learned, they often leave. We meet people for all kinds of reasons and challenges. I have experienced this many times, friendships that initially caused great pain later revealed valuable lessons and strengthened my self-worth. I realised I deserved better.

If this resonates, do not beat yourself up. Continue to be your honest self, even if some truths are difficult for others to see or accept. Remember, this is also their lesson. Those who judge may need to confront their shadow side and nurture the areas within themselves that create hurtful behaviours. Judgement says more about them than about you. Not everyone is meant to stay in your life. Perhaps a chapter closed for a reason. Embrace the change, forgive or accept the circumstance or person, send them love and well wishes, and move on. Holding on will only harm you. Resentment, sadness, and hurt cause emotional distress, which can manifest as mental health issues, chronic illnesses, or disease over time.

Losing friends, disconnecting from family, or feeling betrayed can create profound grief and may take a long time to heal. This is because we attach our energy to situations and people. Until we free ourselves and sever these energetic cords, we continue to carry the energy. Many clients come to me needing to forgive or accept themselves, family members, or friends. Once I focus deeply on clearing these energy frequencies, they are able to move on. They may not forgive everything, but they can at least accept.

Being honest and giving my full attention to this part of my life, helped me learn to give unconditional love to those worthy of it and to set boundaries for those who do not value me. Avoid expecting too much from others. If you feel taken for granted or mistreated, do not remain in that situation. It may be difficult, but in the long run, you will feel better.

Many people are prisoners of their own minds. We all need to break free from chains that hold us back from our authentic selves.

When we pass over to the spirit world, we leave our bodies behind. We release density, all unforgiveness, and pain. We let go of everything that ever affected us. There is no disease in spirit, because we leave behind the dense body and the emotional baggage that causes dis-ease. We do not need to wait until we pass to learn this. We can begin to heal and release now.

Some of my chronic illnesses arose from pain, resentment, and heartache, and I remained unwell until I examined my emotions, cleared stagnant energy, and healed. I discussed this in my chapter on Fibromyalgia and M.E. and how many chronic illnesses stem from unresolved inner issues. I see this repeatedly in clients, and once we address forgiveness, acceptance, and trauma, many symptoms subside.

Unforgiveness breeds bitterness, stress, resentment, anger, hurt, betrayal, and sadness, which takes a toll on the body.

LET IT GO!

The Key to Forgiveness and Acceptance Exercise

Here is a simple and straightforward exercise you can do to help release and free yourself from holding onto unforgiving thoughts or feelings.

- Light a white candle or incense to clear the energy of the room and make it pure for the exercise.

- Find a quiet space and sit with your spine upright and legs crossed.
- With a piece of paper and pen, write down everyone and everything that you need to forgive and be as detailed as you need to be (this can include forgiving yourself).
- Once you have released these issues onto paper, visualise everyone and every situation in a bubble of pink healing light in front of you.
- Visualise yourself letting each person or situation go and forgiving and letting go. (You don't have to condone what a person has done but you can let it go in order to free yourself and the situation from keeping you chained.)
- Then visualise each person's situation slowly floating away inside a pink bubble, rising into the sky until it eventually disappears completely.
- Once you have completed this, take your piece of paper and carefully burn it, either in the garden or over a sink with access to water so that it is done in a safe environment. (By burning the paper, you are no longer holding on to the situation and have released the energy into the ethers.)

Forgiveness and Acceptance Healing Activation

Take a deep breath and connect with the spirit of your body. Say this activation out loud with your hand on your heart. If you feel any resistance, invite the spirit of resistance to move over to the light and into the love of God, then repeat the activation:

Spirit of forgiveness, please enter my heart now.
Spirit of acceptance, I welcome you into every cell in my body.
Spirit of healing, please move through my entire being.

I no longer carry the heaviness of betrayal.
I now carry the lightness and truth of who I am.

I forgive because I choose freedom,
I accept because I choose peace,
I heal because I choose love.
And so it is.

Chapter 23 – Final Reflection

This book began as a vision born from my own search. Throughout times of hardship, I could never find a self-help, spiritual, or healing book that truly spoke to me. One that felt personal, that resonated on an emotional level, and that explained life, healing, and spirituality in a way that was simple, yet profound.

I wanted a book of honesty and authenticity, one that reflected pieces of my own journey. Something that offered gentle guidance, sparked reflection, and inspired you to step into your own power, to move your energy, and to feel comforted in the knowledge that you are never alone.

Above all, I wanted this book to show that no matter how deep your struggles, pain, or challenges may be, it is possible to emerge stronger, wiser, and more whole. This book was created to offer hope, strength, faith, and the understanding that healing is always within reach if you believe in yourself.

From the very first word to the last, I felt guided by the divine, by infinite intelligence, and by my ancestors in spirit. Their presence pushed me forward, gave me clarity, and whispered encouragement when I needed it most. I am also deeply grateful to my clients, whose trust and openness allowed me to grow, to learn, and to share these lessons with you.

Healing is not linear. Life will always present challenges, cycles of ease and difficulty, moments of clarity and moments of confusion. When you feel lost or stagnant, know that these periods are not permanent. Sometimes, life's storms are necessary, they shake us, humble us, and open the way for growth and transformation.

By embracing all parts of ourselves, including the shadowed corners of our being, we uncover truth. This brings us back to balance, to harmony, and to love. I believe that many of our life experiences, even the painful ones, are chosen by our soul to help us grow. How we respond, whether we cling to struggle or choose healing, is entirely up to us.

Many people remain trapped in self-pity, unaware of the power they hold. You are not one of them. You can choose to shift your energy, to release stagnation, and to transform your life. This can happen in a heartbeat, simply by connecting with your spirit guides or creating a personal healing practice.

My hope is that this book reaches the hearts of those who need it, opening minds to alternative ways of healing. To show that our experiences, energy, thoughts, and emotions are not separate from our physical, emotional, and mental wellbeing, they are deeply intertwined.

For a long time, I hesitated to speak openly about spirituality. In Western society, it was often misunderstood or even frowned upon. Yet, even when others judged or doubted me, I was never truly alone. Spirit has always been by my side. It carried me through the darkest moments, and it continues to guide me today.

I now embrace this part of myself, with gratitude and pride. Many people fear the unknown, believing that if they do not conform, something cannot be real. To them, I offer compassion and love.

I am grateful to share my story and the light it can bring. I trust that this book will find those who need it most, guiding them to strength, healing, and joy. My wish is that readers of all ages, from every walk of life, can discover their own power and begin to transform their lives.

Most of all, I hope to educate, nurture, and heal the younger generation, creating a ripple of light and wellbeing that will shape a happier, healthier world. Remember, everything is energy. You have the power to shift it, to move it, and to heal.

Healing is simple. It is available to you here, now, and in this very moment.

With love, light, and blessings,

Hannah Olivia.

About the Author

Hannah Olivia is the creator of *The Girl Healer*™, a global spiritual brand with hundreds of clients around the world, including some celebrities.

A qualified Reiki Master and Rahanni Celestial Healing Master, she has also studied Crystal Healing, Angelic Healing, Spiritual Healing, and Shamanic Quantum Healing. Trained as both a psychic and a medium, she spent two years in an intimate circle dedicated to advancing mediumship.

With a degree in English and Journalism, Hannah blends her love of storytelling with her passion for deep, transformative healing. Her mission is to guide others in healing their inner world so they may create a brighter, more fulfilling outer one.

Be Healed, Be Happy is her debut book, inspired by years of guiding people through profound emotional, spiritual, and energetic transformation. She is also the host of *The Healing Hour* podcast, where she shares wisdom, insights, and conversations designed to awaken personal growth and spiritual connection.

Follow Hannah Olivia on:

Instagram @thegirlhealer
X @thegirlhealer
Facebook The Girl Healer
TikTok @thegirlhealer
Threads thegirlhealer
Twitter @Thegirlhealer
website www.thegirlhealer.com

Printed in Dunstable, United Kingdom

68877238R00111